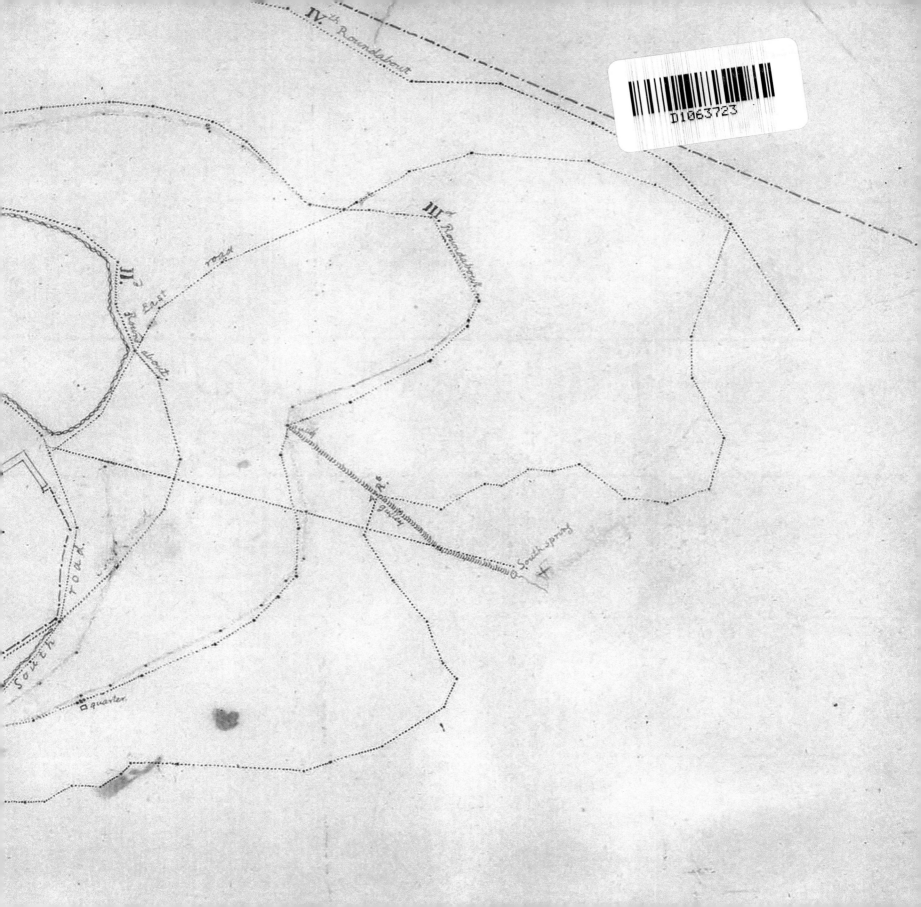

Thomas Jefferson's
MONTICELLO

Thomas Jefferson's
MONTICELLO

THOMAS JEFFERSON FOUNDATION, INC.

	August			
	Wormley 2 doz eggs	P.	1	6
3	Sunday			
	Frank 20 chickens		10	
	Frederic 12 dit		6	
	9 ducks		9	
	Warner 13 chickens		6	6
	Squire 2 doz apples			
	1 doz cucumbers } P	3		
	1 lb of bees wax }			
	Ned & Billy 1 doz cucumbers }			
	9 eggs }	1	6	
	1 watermelon }			
	Lewis 3 doz eggs	P.	2	3
	Gilly 1½ doz eggs		1	1½
	3 lb soap old debt		3	
	Barnaby 1 doz eggs - - - -			9
	snaps - - -			

Library of Congress Cataloging-in-Publication Data

Thomas Jefferson's Monticello
     p. cm.
    Includes bibliographical references (p.   ) and index.
    ISBN 978-0-615-83006-3
      1. Monticello (Va.)—Pictorial works. 2. Jefferson, Thomas, 1743-1826—Homes and
haunts—Virginia—Albemarle County—Pictorial works. 3. Monticello (Va.)—History. I.
Thomas Jefferson Foundation, Inc.

    E332.74.T48 2012
    975.5'482—dc21

                                          2002016138

This book was made possible by support from the
Martin S. and Luella Davis Publications Endowment.

Edited and coordinated by Gaye Wilson and Sharon McElroy
Designed by Keith Damiani
Printed in China by Four Color Printing Group, Louisville, Kentucky

Distributed by:

MONTICELLO

Thomas Jefferson Foundation, Inc.
Post Office Box 316
Charlottesville, VA 22902

HGFED

Contents

Foreword

Philosopher, revolutionary, president, scientist, diplomat, innovator, educator, farmer, oenophile, and epicure. Author of the Declaration of Independence and lifelong slaveholder.

Thomas Jefferson was an essential architect of American life. Two centuries later, his genius, complexity, and commitment to progress still captivate our attention.

Some 450,000 people make the pilgrimage to Monticello each year, and millions more visit virtually. They follow in the footsteps of generations of visitors, drawn to a little mountain in Charlottesville by a quintessentially American story. This was true even as Jefferson was shaping the first chapter of his masterpiece.

President Franklin Delano Roosevelt's motorcade enters Monticello on July 4, 1936.

In 1782, the Marquis de Chastellux, a member of the French Academy and an officer in General Rochambeau's army, arrived at Monticello on Jefferson's thirty-ninth birthday. Chastellux was among the first notable foreign visitors to Monticello, and he recorded his impressions in a travel diary that was later widely published: "[W]e may safely aver, that Mr. Jefferson is the first American who has consulted the fine arts to know how he should shelter himself from the weather."

Fast forward to a twentieth-century dignitary's visit. On July 4, 1936, President Franklin Delano Roosevelt

offered reflections on Monticello in a speech he delivered from the West Portico: "More than any historic home in America, Monticello appeals to me as an expression of the personality of its builder. In the design, not of the whole alone, but of every room ... there speaks ready capacity for detail and, above all, creative genius."

Thus began a tradition of welcoming distinguished persons to speak on what Jefferson called "the great birthday of our Republic." From architect I. M. Pei to Madeleine Albright, the first woman to serve as secretary of state, Monticello's roster of July Fourth speakers is an American tapestry. Since Roosevelt, three other U.S. presidents have delivered the Independence Day address: Harry S. Truman, Gerald R. Ford, and George W. Bush.

Just before sunset on February 10, 2014, our forty-fourth president brought French president François Hollande to Monticello—the most distinguished French guest to visit the mountaintop since Jefferson welcomed his old comrade, the Marquis de Lafayette, in 1824. At the state dinner that followed, President Hollande described Jefferson and Monticello as "beautiful symbols of the ties that unite us."

ABOVE LEFT · President George W. Bush welcomes new citizens following his address for Monticello's forty-sixth Independence Day Celebration and Naturalization Ceremony, July 4, 2008.

ABOVE RIGHT · French president François Hollande with Leslie Greene Bowman and President Barack Obama in Jefferson's Cabinet at Monticello.

ABOVE • John Lewis, U.S. congressman from Georgia, received the Thomas Jefferson Foundation Medal in Citizen Leadership in 2015.

BELOW • Philanthropist David M. Rubenstein, co-founder and co-executive Chairman of The Carlyle Group, whose transformational gifts to Monticello launched the Mountaintop Project in 2014. Rubenstein is pictured here with Monticello trustee Jon Meacham (LEFT), Pulitzer Prize–winning author and historian.

Whether undertaken by two presidents or two dozen schoolchildren, the journey to Monticello is a shared American experience. At the end of a winding mountain road sits a house and plantation that invites a conversation about who we are, where we came from, and the country we might aspire to become. The Thomas Jefferson Foundation has been dedicated to making this journey possible since 1923, through an evergreen mission of education and preservation. In addition to Monticello and the mountaintop landscape, our stewardship now includes 2,600 acres of the original 5,000 that Jefferson owned in Albemarle County.

Today, Monticello's visitors encounter a United Nations World Heritage Site and National Historic Landmark, where the power of place combines with the power of Jefferson's world-changing ideas.

On what was once a working plantation, the paradox of slavery stands in stark relief to the ideals of liberty that Jefferson embedded in the Declaration of Independence. The Mountaintop Project (2014–18), a recent multiyear initiative catalyzed by a gift from philanthropist David M. Rubenstein, has further revealed the history of slavery at Monticello—and allowed us to present the mountaintop as those who lived here would have known it. Along Mulberry Row, once a hub of work and domestic life for the enslaved, one finds real and virtual re-creations of lost buildings. The South Wing is another place to hear the stories of individuals who labored on the mountain, and to grapple with the legacies of slavery that are still shaping our society today. Importantly, all of this work has been informed by over twenty-five years of oral histories shared by the descendants of Monticello's enslaved families. This ongoing project, called *Getting Word*, has grown into a significant oral history archive.

We invite you to embark on your own journey here, and to join us in bringing history forward into dialogue. In the words of Pulitzer Prize–winning historian Jon Meacham—at Monticello you are "as close as you can get to having a conversation with Thomas Jefferson."

—LESLIE GREENE BOWMAN
President, Thomas Jefferson Foundation

TOP RIGHT · President Harry S. Truman gives the Independence Day address from Monticello's West Portico on July 4, 1947.

BOTTOM RIGHT · Daniel P. Jordan escorts the emperor and empress of Japan through Monticello, June 15, 1994.

Preface

"I am as happy nowhere else and in no other society, and all my wishes end, where I hope my days will end, at Monticello," Thomas Jefferson wrote to his neighbor George Gilmer in the summer of 1787. At the time, Jefferson was three years in France serving as the minister from the United States. His Paris residence, the Hôtel de Langeac, was situated in a relatively new but fashionable part of the city. The house was sumptuous, with a sophisticated and spacious layout, complete with indoor privies. The manicured grounds finished the effect, providing Jefferson with the highest standard of living he had ever known and would ever know. Yet despite the splendor of his surroundings, and as much as he loved French culture—the music, the architecture, the cuisine, the people—Jefferson held fast to his idealized vision of his mountaintop home. Here was where he felt truly complete and at ease; the place that most effectively announced to the world the aspirations he had for himself and, as the years wore on, the aspirations he had for the country he helped to found.

In later years, during his tenures in national political office, Jefferson spoke of Monticello rapturously as a refuge from the "miseries" of political life in the various early national capitals where he served in the American government. Those places—New York, Philadelphia, and Washington—were cities of different sizes and characters, but to Jefferson, they all embodied chaos and discord. Monticello was for him, everything those places were not: a place of peace, beauty, order, and the enveloping warmth of family. In truth, however, Jefferson's negative response to these sites of public office, and determination to cling to his ideal of Monticello, were not simply the products of his hatred of the vicissitudes of political life. Long before he became a public figure, Jefferson showed signs of having a deep longing for a home that satisfied his quest for solitude and a degree of separation from others. Although he appreciated his neighbors (generally), he needed to keep a proper distance from them. A home on a mountaintop was a perfect solution. He had dreamed of that as a young boy, growing up at Shadwell, situated near the base of the 868-foot-high mountain that he would name Monticello. In 1768, he arranged to have the top of the mountain leveled; arduous work done by hired enslaved laborers. He brought his young bride, Martha, to live there in 1772 before he built the first version of Monticello, the couple residing in a one-room building that Jefferson lived in briefly as a bachelor. Because no letters between the couple are extant, we do not know what, if any, of his vision for the finished house Thomas shared with Martha. We do know that at the time of her death in 1782, the house was still unfinished.

When Jefferson built the second incarnation of Monticello, and planned the exterior and interior, he took cues from things he had learned during his five-year stay in Paris and from studying the works of the Italian architect Andrea Palladio. Both fired his imagination, putting a now more worldly man into a more sophisticated version of a home. The Hôtel de Salm in Paris, with which Jefferson said he was "smitten," inspired him to build a house with a dome. Palladian architecture appealed to his love of symmetry, which he tried to reproduce at Monticello. His obsession with privacy led to one conspicuous exception. During his first term as president, Jefferson upset his house's balance by having enclosed porches attached to the southern and eastern parts of the terrace outside of his bedroom. They were built with blinds that could be opened and closed at Jefferson's will—leaving as much, or as little, of a view into his living quarters as he chose. The porticles (as he called them) were particularly useful during his retirement, when throngs of uninvited visitors trekked up the mountain to wander the grounds and catch a glimpse of the Great Man. Like the architect who designed it, the house's exterior hides much. What appears to be a one-story structure is, in fact, multistory, with a far larger and more complicated interior, than its exterior suggests. Monticello is, indeed, a form of autobiography.

Jefferson designed his personal living quarters in Monticello along the lines of the space he had known in the Hôtel de Langeac. This was his "sanctum sanctorum," where he spent "much of his time … engaged in correspondence and reading and writing." It was a place of self-fashioning, where Jefferson imagined the kind of man he wanted to be and wanted to present to the world. Even loved ones knew that he was to be left alone during large segments of the day to produce what would become a voluminous body of writing; not only letters, but plantation records, architectural designs, a garden book, and memoranda of daily purchases and transactions. At work's end, Jefferson would emerge from "his office" to share meals and go riding.

Monticello was not just a place where Jefferson acted the role of gentleman farmer and participated in the Republic of Letters. His ornamental farm was a slave plantation. He shared this space with hundreds of enslaved men, women, and children who worked in the fields at the home plantation Monticello, and the other quarter farms bordering it—Tufton, Shadwell, and Lego. Many of these individuals and families spent more time at Monticello than Jefferson, who was away for long periods of time on the public's business. It is often written that Jefferson, embarrassed by slavery, attempted to hide enslaved people at Monticello by directing them through obscure passageways as they served Jefferson and his guests. But there was no way Jefferson could hide slavery from himself or from his visitors. He interacted with enslaved people each day. Mulberry Row, where enslaved workers worked and lived, is adjacent to Jefferson's living quarters. He would have heard their voices and the sound of their work; he would have seen them moving about the area. Visitors commented on the contrast between the tiny log homes of the enslaved on one side of the road and the elegant mansion on the other.

Monticello was always a work in progress, never quite finished, always in need of repair. Jefferson continued to entertain while living in the midst of the chaos of building. In 1794, he wryly told his old teacher and friend George Wythe that he was "living in a brick kiln." The final form of the house, with its signature dome, had taken shape by the time Jefferson retired from the presidency in 1809. That same year, Martha (Patsy) Randolph, his surviving daughter with his wife, moved her family to Monticello, permanently joining in one place two family lines: Jefferson's eldest daughter and her children, and his children with his wife's enslaved half sister, Sarah (Sally) Hemings.

From Jefferson's retirement until his death, Monticello teemed with children, grandchildren, visitors—invited and not. Jefferson was the sun around which everyone at Monticello orbited. Under these circumstances, he zealously protected his privacy, imposing an exacting schedule that limited access to him. Privileged visitors were drawn into the family circle, gathered in the parlor or dining room for conversation, music, or fine food. They waited for these occasions in a hall that was a veritable museum, filled with treasures Jefferson had brought from France displayed alongside maps, artifacts from Native Americans, and items from archaeological digs. Visitors were seldom disappointed, for the patriarch made each person he met feel special. One remembered that Jefferson offered "instruction like light from an inexhaustible solar fountain, he seemed continually to be asking, instead of giving information."

In his last years, the profoundly private man who dreamed of a home away from it all loomed ever larger in the national imagination. "An immense influx of visitors" made the "pilgrimage" up the little mountain to pay their respects to him and the house that was already beginning to be seen as a form of monument. He often escaped for weeks at a time to Poplar Forest, 90 miles away from Monticello. That his private home should become a national shrine was not an outcome that the dreaming young Virginian/British subject could have foreseen when he first thought to live on a mountain. Nor could he have foreseen that he would become the embodiment of what has been called the American paradox of liberty and slavery. But, in nearly all important ways, Jefferson's lofty aspirations for himself, his home, and then the country he helped to create—along with the ways in which he fell short—are inextricably linked to the American story.

—ANNETTE GORDON-REED

Author of The Hemingses of Monticello, *winner of the Pulitzer Prize and the National Book Award, and the Charles Warren Professor of American Legal History at Harvard Law School and the Carol K. Pforzheimer Professor at the Radcliffe Institute of Advanced Study at Harvard University*

—PETER S. ONUF

Thomas Jefferson Foundation Professor of History, Emeritus, Corcoran Department of History, University of Virginia, and Senior Research Fellow at the Robert H. Smith International Center for Jefferson Studies, and Mellon Distinguished Scholar in Residence, American Antiquarian Society, 2018

The Plantation
A DAY IN THE LIFE

By LUCIA STANTON
Shannon Senior Research Historian Emeritus at Monticello

ABOVE • Jefferson's notes on fields at Monticello and the rotation of crops for each. He experimented with agricultural methods that improved the soil and reduced the damage from the many years of single-crop tobacco farming.

OPPOSITE • Mulberry Row's Storehouse for Iron was built circa 1793 to house a tinsmithing shop. Later it was used as a slave dwelling and nailery. It was reconstructed in 2014 as part of the Mountaintop Project.

The summer of 1814 was a time of national anxiety. "We are all on the alert as to the fate of Washington," Jefferson wrote to a neighbor on August 27, not yet aware that three days earlier the British army had entered the federal city and set fire to its public buildings.[1] Even in the midst of war, however, life on the Monticello plantation proceeded according to its usual unchanging rhythms, and its seventy-one-year-old proprietor continued to follow his own daily regimen. While Jefferson's precise actions on any one day can never be fully recovered, his monumental archive provides sufficient information about the activities of August 1814 to evoke a typical plantation day in that month.

After a morning committed to his burdensome correspondence, Jefferson devoted the middle of the day to outdoor activities that satisfied his belief in the importance of daily physical exercise as well as his need to supervise his plantation operations and an enslaved workforce of 140 individuals. He first walked along Mulberry Row, the hub of plantation activity, to monitor the activities of his enslaved tradesmen. The highly skilled ironworkers, Joseph Fossett and Moses Hern, were in the blacksmith shop, attaching an iron moldboard—made to Jefferson's own innovative design—to a large wooden plow. They had been unable to make nails since they used the last supply of nailrod, shipped before the British blockaded the Chesapeake ports.

In the joinery, John Hemmings awaited Jefferson's orders for a set of bookshelves. His brother Peter Hemings was preparing equipment in the malthouse for the autumn brewing of beer.

Jefferson stopped at the textile workshop, a stone building that still stands on Mulberry Row. This was normally the domain of his daughter Martha Randolph, but he stopped to ask fourteen-year-old Israel Gillette, who was both a stable groom and a carder in the shop, to return to the stable to saddle his horse. Gillette and three other slave boys prepared the fiber for the spinners, five women and teenaged girls who operated machines with twenty-four to forty-eight spindles. The spinners produced yarn of wool, cotton, and hemp that was woven into

ABOVE • Nails, nailrod, and nailmaking tools excavated on Mulberry Row recall an industry that was pursued by enslaved men and boys at Monticello for thirty years.

RIGHT • Jefferson recorded how much iron nailrod his enslaved nailmakers used, how many nails they made, and calculated the profit earned from each slave.

Analysis of work from Jan. 1. to Mar. 31 1796.

	rod ℔	nails	profit £	days	daily profit d
Isaac	539.8	507.1	11–13–3	47	59.5
Moses	563.1	526.1	12–6–4	62	47.7
Joe	352.3	326.8	7–12–10	43	42.6
Shepherd	480.7	438.2	10–3–3	67.	36.4
Jamey	465.1	420.6	9–13–4	65	35.7
Wormely	488.8	452.4	10–12–4	68	37.4
Barnaby	352.2	317.9	7–8–5	50	35.6
Burwell	429.5	392.1	9–6–5	66	33.9

The stone chimney of the Joiner's Shop stands as a reminder of woodworking on Mulberry Row. It is one of only four buildings to survive (all or in part) of the more than 22 original structures that once lined Monticello's busiest thoroughfare. Joiners James Dinsmore and John Hemmings and other free and enslaved craftsmen fashioned decorative woodwork for the house and furniture.

ABOVE • Benjamin H. Latrobe, *An Overseer Doing His Duty near Fredericksburg, Virginia*, watercolor on paper, ca. 1798. As was typical on Virginia plantations, enslaved laborers at Monticello worked from dawn to dark, six days a week. Some tended crops and livestock, while others played essential roles on Mulberry Row as carpenters, blacksmiths, weavers, and cooks or in the house as butlers, maids, or nursemaids.

LEFT • Archaeological excavations along Mulberry Row unearthed evidence of clothing construction among the enslaved community that included needles, pins, and thimbles, and buttons punched from cow bones.

ABOVE • Restored in 2017 as a part of the Mountaintop Project, this two-room stone structure, erected circa 1775, is the third oldest structure at Monticello. It alternately housed hired white and enslaved workers. After Monticello's construction was completed, it contained the Textile Workshop where the women and children turned cotton, hemp, and wool into cloth for the entire enslaved community.

LEFT • A modern view of Mulberry Row looking from the stone chimney of the Joiner's Shop toward the restored Textile Workshop.

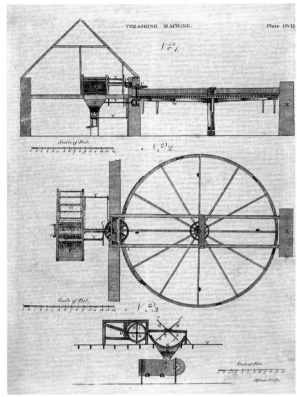

THRASHING MACHINE.

cloth by Mary Hern and Dolly on looms with flying shuttles.

After Jefferson mounted his bay horse Bremo, he rode down the mountain through pastures where a flock of Barbary Broadtail sheep was tended by a young shepherd, aided by a French sheepdog. A mile from the mountaintop, Jefferson reached the Monticello farm quarters, where he and overseer Edmund Bacon discussed the prospects for the corn crop. Continuing down the mountain to the Rivanna River, Jefferson entered the River Field, where enslaved foreman James Hern and several other enslaved men and women were clearing the field of briars and stones before the October planting of wheat. Jefferson paused at his new sawmill at the edge of the field, where the head carpenter, a free white man named Roland Goodman, was supervising three enslaved men repairing the waterwheel that drove the mill, and pondered a solution to the problem of insufficient water from the sawmill canal.

Low water in the Rivanna River made fording easy. Jefferson crossed over to Lego farm, one of the quarter farms that made up the 5,000-acre plantation. Here overseer Elijah Ham was directing a group of enslaved laborers cutting clover in the Triangle Field. Ham reported that the threshing machine, which had processed over 150 bushels of the summer's wheat crop the day before, needed repair. Jefferson proceeded downstream, along a canal beside the river to the Shadwell quarter farm. On the opposite bank, on the Tufton quarter farm, he could see enslaved coalburner David Hern carefully stacking split sticks of wood to make a dome-shaped kiln, which he would cover with turf and set alight. This kiln would produce 974 bushels of charcoal, fuel for the forges of the blacksmiths on Mulberry Row and some of the stoves in the house.

View across a field of Black-eyed Susans (*Rudbeckia hirta*) at Jefferson's Tufton Farm, with Montalto in the distance.

Plate XXI.

JEFFERSON'S MILL AT SHADWELL.

ABOVE • Jefferson's merchant mill at Shadwell, completed in 1807, processed local wheat into flour, which was then shipped down the Rivanna and James Rivers to market in Richmond. The mill no longer stands today but is shown as illustrated in a magazine from 1853.

LEFT • Jefferson's large merchant mill was similar to this one, with two pairs of millstones and the latest milling machinery patented by Oliver Evans.

LOSSING=BARRITT

Jefferson had now reached the bustling site of his millworks at Shadwell, where two mills filled the air with the crashing sounds of gears and machinery. He passed a mule cart, driven by enslaved wagoner Jerry, loaded with cornmeal for the main house. At the toll mill, which ground grain for home use, he agreed to buy a dozen guinea fowl from the free white miller, Youen Carden. Jefferson had leased out the larger mill, which ground his and his neighbors' wheat for market. This merchant mill had two pair of millstones and the most up-to-date milling machinery, patented by Oliver Evans. Its tenants purchased their flour barrels from Jefferson's coopers' shops, where he dismounted to talk to two slaves, Barnaby Gillette and Nace, about the need for increasing production from four to six barrels a day. Normally, the market flour was shipped down the Rivanna and James Rivers to Richmond; however, Jefferson's flour from the 1813 wheat crop was still there. He wrote that due to the war, "none can be sold at any price."

Jefferson rode farther downstream before crossing back to the south side of the Rivanna and the small town of Milton, more than three miles from where he began on Mulberry Row. After stopping to negotiate a contract with a man who wished to cut firewood on his lands surrounding the town, he ended his outward journey on the slopes behind Milton with a bit of quail shooting. In his daily combination of exercise and plantation management, Jefferson probably rode as much as ten miles, never leaving his own property.

The Land

In August 1814, Jefferson's Albemarle County plantation contained 5,375 acres on both sides of the Rivanna River. At the Monticello home farm and two quarter farms, Tufton and Lego, almost a thousand acres were under cultivation. Jefferson

FOLLOWING PAGES • Montalto (upper left), the "high mountain," rises 410 feet above Monticello. It remained timbered during Jefferson's lifetime and was a source for hardwoods and a grazing site for cattle and pigs. Jefferson expressed a preference "for good woodland beef, which is the best possible."

had deeded the Shadwell farm to his grandson in 1813, excluding the Shadwell Mill, which he retained, and he did not grow crops on Montalto, the mountain rising above Monticello to the southwest. Its forest cover provided a source of hardwoods and woodland grazing for pigs and cattle.

Jefferson had inherited three thousand acres from his father, Peter Jefferson, in 1764. For almost thirty years afterward, he followed the usual course of Virginia plantation owners. With the labor of slaves, he raised tobacco as his main cash crop, which he sold to a Scottish mercantile firm, and grew Indian corn to feed his laborers and livestock. In his *Notes on the State of Virginia*, he condemned this mode of agriculture, writing that the cultivation of tobacco was "productive of infinite wretchedness." Raising a tobacco crop and getting it to market required exhausting labor over eighteen months: planting, transplanting, weeding, topping, suckering, deworming, cutting, curing, stripping, stemming, and finally, packing into hogsheads to be shipped to inspection warehouses in Richmond. "The men and animals on these farms are badly fed," Jefferson observed, "and the earth is

In 1814, Jefferson owned about 5,375 acres of land in Albemarle County, divided between the quarter farms of Monticello, Tufton, and Lego.

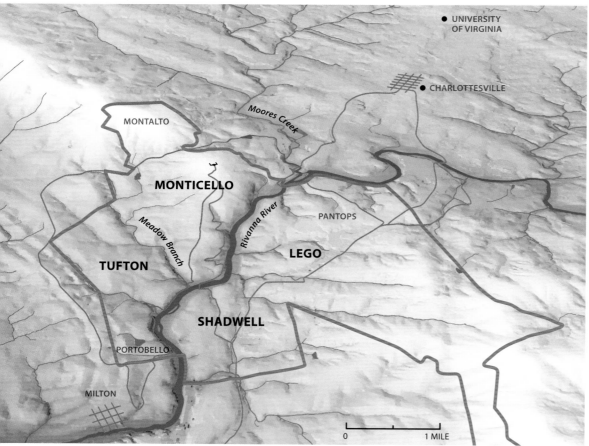

rapidly impoverished."[2]

Nevertheless, it was not until the early 1790s that Jefferson began to transform Monticello from a tobacco plantation to a wheat farm. He banished tobacco from his rotation (except for occasional crops planted when prices were particularly high) and raised wheat as the staple crop. In this period, Jefferson was inspired by British and American agricultural reformers. He studied their improvements in books and periodicals, at demonstrations of machinery and livestock, and in conversation or correspondence with the best practical farmers.

Jefferson began his own agricultural reforms on his retirement as secretary of state in 1794. Faced with the "degradation" of his lands from the "slovenly business of tobacco-making," he embarked on a kind of rescue operation that focused on the restoration of the soil.[3] Describing himself as the "most ardent farmer" in Virginia, he adopted a seven-year schedule of crop rotation, incorporating three years of the soil-improving legume red clover, as well as wheat, rye, potatoes, and field peas.[4] He tried to minimize the planting of soil-depleting Indian corn, but was never able to find satisfactory substitutes for this basic necessity. By 1809, Jefferson committed himself to regular applications of gypsum plaster to lower the acidity of his soil; dung was never a major Monticello fertilizer, as cattle and hogs roamed widely in the

From the 1790s, wheat replaced tobacco as the main market crop of the Monticello plantation. The annual wheat harvest took place at the end of June, bringing together over sixty enslaved laborers form the age of nine to sixty-nine. The strongest men mowed the wheat with cradle scythes, while women and boys gathered it into sheaves. The 1868 engraving above, entitled *Stacking Hay*, depicts African American field workers harvesting wheat in rural Virginia.

surrounding woods, fenced out of the areas of tillage.

The conversion to grain cultivation required a greatly expanded program of plowing, which brought its associated problems. Soil erosion accelerated and, in 1795, Jefferson wrote of "the ravages committed by the rains. ... I imagine we never lost more soil than this summer."[5] It was only the use of contour plowing, introduced in Albemarle County about 1804 by Jefferson's son-in-law Thomas Mann Randolph, that finally helped to arrest the terrible loss of topsoil. On the Monticello plantation there were plows in the fields, weather permitting, almost every working day of the year. This perpetual round of plowing required horses, mules, and oxen in top condition.

In August 1814, there were 18 horses, 8 mules, 71 head of cattle, 178 hogs, and 150 sheep on the five-thousand-acre plantation. While president, Jefferson had become keenly interested in the breeding of both sheep and hogs. He introduced the Guinea hog to increase the weights of the scrawny beasts that ranged the Monticello woodlands, and he eventually had three distinct breeds of sheep at Monticello and his Bedford County plantation, Poplar Forest. He preferred the "delicious" meat of the Tunis breed from North Africa for his table and had a cross-bred flock of Spanish and American descent for wool.[6] He also tried to raise the merino sheep, whose export from Spain had been prohibited for centuries. The first shipments of merinos to the United States brought on a national case of "Merino mania" in 1809 and 1810, when purebred rams brought prices as high as one thousand dollars. Southern plantation owners like Jefferson soon learned that the merinos' extremely fine fleece was unsuitable for weaving the coarse cloth they issued to their enslaved laborers.

The multiple activities of a mixed grain and livestock operation had replaced the single-minded, labor-intensive pursuit of a crop of tobacco. Along with this diversity

Jefferson became interested in sheep breeding while president and thought the fine-fleeced Spanish merino breed would revolutionize textile production in the South. He hoped to benefit his state by donating rams from his own flock to each county. Virginians, however, quickly lost interest in the merino, "preferring," as Jefferson said, "those breeds giving most wool to what gives the finest." For the table, Jefferson singled out the Barbary Broadtail (now Tunis) sheep for praise.

came a need for a variety of vehicles and more complicated machinery, like threshing machines and grain drills, that demanded frequent maintenance and expertise in operation. Jefferson actively sought to spread word of these latest agricultural improvements to his fellow countrymen. In the 1790s, he had refined his design for a "moldboard of least resistance" for a plow, communicating its benefits through letters, diagrams, and models that he sent to both Americans and Europeans. He imported a model of the recently patented Scottish threshing machine, "to save the labours of my countrymen."[7] Hoping his neighbors would profit by his example, he had three machines based on this model constructed at Monticello.

The sale of an annual crop of wheat or flour was dependent on events taking place hundreds and often thousands of miles away. The Embargo Act of 1807, the War of 1812, and, finally, the severe agricultural depression after 1818 all adversely affected Jefferson's income from his plantation. "I am not fit to be a farmer with the kind of labour that we have," he wrote in 1799, discouraged by the difficulty of managing his enslaved farm laborers so that productivity was achieved without cruelty.[8] His absences in public service defeated his plan for the systematic improvement of his own farms, and he never accommodated his vision of free labor and family farms to the realities of slavery. But Jefferson continued to be the most articulate spokesman for a nation of independent farmers—patriotic, industrious, and self-governing. Agriculture, he wrote in 1817, is "the happiest [employment] we can follow, and the most important to our country."[9]

Jefferson received a gold medal from a French agricultural society for his improved moldboard for a plow, now considered his one true invention. He conceived his design for the "moldboard of least resistance" while traveling through eastern France in 1788. Woodworker Robert L. Self and blacksmith Peter Ross used Jefferson's drawings to make this full-scale model of a barshare plow with a Jeffersonian moldboard.

Monticello		the farm	Tufton	Lego
Betty Brown.	Nance	Abram.	Abram junr.	?
Mary.	Peter Hemings	Doll.	Bagwell	Bar
Billy B.	Sally	Barnaby	Minerva	Cha
Burwell	Beverly	Stannard	Willis	🕮
Caesar.	Harriet	Davy.	Archy	Dav
Critta	Madison	Isabel	Jordan	Eve.
Davy junr.	Eston.	Thrimston.	Ben	Jo.
Fanny.	Wormly	Polly. Charles.	Lilly	Bu
Ellen	Ursula & Louisa	Isaac.	Lucy	Evel
Jenny.	Joe	James	Dick B.	Jam
Ned	Anne	Cretia	Dick. Ned's	Rach
Gill	Dolly	Johnny.	Esther	Joe
Israel	Cornelius	Randal	Lindsay	La
Dolly	Thomas.	Henry	Sucky	Gl
Joe		Milly	Isaiah	Wa
Edy		Lilburne	Jerry junr.	Ed.
~~James~~		Matilda.	John B.	Lucyb
Maria.		Band.	Virginia	Ro
Patsy		James. Lewis.	Robert	Sa
Betsy		James. Ned's	Amanda.	M
Peter.		Terry	Maria & Martin	Milly
John Hemings		Isabel	Marshal.	Sar
John gardener.		Jupiter.	Mary. Bagwell's	Mo
		Amy.		
		Jenny. L's		
		Jenny. Ned.		
		Moses		

Slavery at Monticello

Jefferson was heir to men, women, and children as well as land. At Monticello he perpetuated the same slave labor system that his father had practiced before him. Enslaved men and women cultivated the crops; cared for the livestock; drove the carts and wagons; built and maintained the fences, farm buildings, and machinery; and made thousands of yards of cloth. Their activities were supervised by overseers, mostly local white men hired by the year. While Jefferson attempted to balance the humane treatment of slaves with the hard work needed to produce income, there were recorded incidents of brutality from some of the overseers and stewards he employed on his farms.

From his father's estate, Jefferson had inherited about 20 people, who by 1774 had, through the birth of children, increased to 52. In that year, a further 135 enslaved African Americans became his property after the division of the estate of his father-in-law, John Wayles. Thereafter, Jefferson owned in any one year around two hundred slaves, about two-thirds of them resident on the Monticello plantation while the rest lived at Poplar Forest in Bedford County.

By 1814, there were almost 175 people living on the Monticello plantation: on the home farm, at Tufton on the south side of the Rivanna River, and at Lego on the north side. Besides Jefferson's white family, this total included three overseers, the head carpenter, the miller, and their families, and nearly 140 enslaved African American men, women, and children. At the farms, the workers were in the fields from dawn to dusk, six days a week, while the older women cared for the young

ABOVE • Lucy Cottrell, who was probably born at Monticello, holds Charlotte Elizabeth Blatterman about 1850. Lucy's mother, Dorothea (Dolly) Cottrell, was an enslaved domestic servant in the household of Jefferson's daughter Martha J. Randolph and thus lived at Monticello after 1809. Both Dolly and Lucy Cottrell were freed by the Blatterman family of Maysville, Kentucky, in 1855.

OPPOSITE • In 1774, Jefferson inherited 135 slaves, in addition to the 52 he already owned, from his father-in-law, John Wayles. He then inaugurated what he called his Farm Book by making a list of the enslaved men, women, and children at Monticello and his other plantations in Virginia.

children and did the cooking. The farm laborers worked, according to the Monticello custom, in "gangs" of half men, half women, and both men and women drove the plows.

About sixty enslaved African Americans lived on or near the top of Monticello Mountain, along Mulberry Row, or in scattered locations on its slopes. They were the house servants, the blacksmiths and carpenters, grooms and gardeners, the carters and wag-oners, and the textile workers. Mulberry Row was the hub of plantation activity and comprised more than twenty workshops, storehouses, and dwellings for free and enslaved workers.

The level of skills in these workshops was remarkably high. As Jefferson wrote in 1816, "To be independant for the comforts of life we must fabricate them ourselves."[10] Monticello's location far from the markets of large towns or cities required a significant degree of self-sufficiency. Especially during the periods of construction on the main house, Jefferson brought to the mountaintop artisans with a wide array of skills, free men recently arrived from Ireland, Scotland, and Germany, as well as Americans. The blacksmith William Stewart,

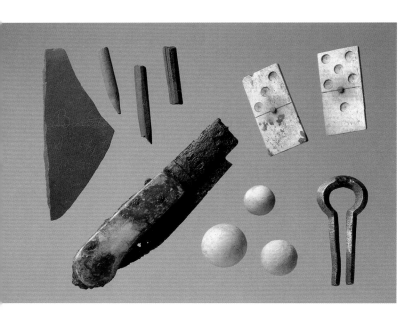

Artifacts excavated along Mulberry Row, including a piece of slate with the fragmentary words of a writing lesson on it, recall the leisure time activities of the slaves.

weaver William Maclure, carpenters James Dinsmore and John Neilson, and stonecutter John Gorman practiced their trades at Monticello and trained enslaved men and women, who in turn passed these skills on to other members of their families and community.

Jefferson's free overseers and workmen were paid annual wages between $100 and $275 and given allowances of bacon and cornmeal as well as housing. The enslaved men and women were unpaid, except for occasional "premiums" for the coopers, charcoalburners, and blacksmiths as an incentive to increase productivity. The weekly food rations for each adult consisted of a peck of cornmeal, a half pound of pork or pickled beef, and four salted fish. Their annual cloth distributions included both a summer and winter suit of clothes, plus a blanket every three years and occasional hats, socks, and shoes. Evidently no furnishings, except for certain cooking utensils, were provided for their cabins.

It is evident that, in their free time, many of Monticello's enslaved men and women continued to work in order to supplement their allotments of food, clothing, and furnishings. In the evenings and on Sundays, they tended their gardens and poultry yards, raising extra vegetables and chickens to sell to their master; they fished and hunted to vary their diet; they made furniture and clothing for their own households and items like brooms and wooden pails to sell; they also performed tasks outside their working hours for which Jefferson paid them.

In the intervals of after-hours labor to earn money, care for their families, and improve their living conditions, the enslaved men and women of Monticello activated a web of connections that bound them together into a community. Sunday was a time for visiting among the quarter farms of the plantation or beyond its borders, for which written permission from master or overseer was usually required. Nights and Sundays were also full of music and dancing, sports, religious observances, and the occasional midnight excursion in search of possum or wild honey. A number of Jefferson's slaves were eager to read and write, and they sought an education from their relatives or from members of Jefferson's family. As one former Monticello slave recalled, "I learned to read by inducing the white children to teach me the letters."[11]

Documentary records and oral history reveal strong family and community ties among Monticello's enslaved African Americans, where skills and values were passed from generation to generation. David and Isabel Hern had fifty-five children and grandchildren who lived in bondage at Monticello. Hern was a skilled woodworker and wheelwright and his wife was a domestic servant. Of their sons, James was a foreman of labor, Moses a blacksmith, David a wagoner, and Thrimston a carpenter and stonecutter. Their daughter Lily was a farm laborer, while Edith Hern Fossett learned French cookery at the President's House (as the White House was then called) and was head cook at Monticello for many years.

Over forty members of another family lived at Monticello. Edward and Jane Gillette, whose marriage linked the Jefferson and Wayles populations, were both farm workers. Their daughters Fanny and Susan were nursemaids and their son Barnaby

Monticello slaves received a weekly ration (partially shown above), which included a peck of cornmeal, three to four fish, and a half pound of fatback pork or pickled beef per adult. To supplement it, slaves worked at night and on Sundays, growing food and raising chickens to sell to the Jefferson family and in Charlottesville's market for cash payments. Money went to buy personal items and household goods.

The worlds of the house and plantation converged in the Monticello kitchen. In 1814, the vegetables grown by head gardener Wormley Hughes and meat raised by foreman James Hern were transformed into meals for Jefferson and his family by enslaved women and boys. The head cooks were Edith Hern Fossett and her sister-in-law Frances Gillette Hern, while Israel Gillette and Robert Colbert worked under them as scullions.

was a cooper. His younger brothers Gill, James, and Israel worked in the Monticello house and kitchen and drove Jefferson's carriage. The recollections of Israel Gillette, who took the surname Jefferson after he gained his freedom, were published in 1873.

One family, the Grangers, which Jefferson purchased in 1773, held positions of great importance. George Granger Sr. was a foreman of labor who rose to occupy the post of overseer, the only enslaved man to do so. His wife Ursula was a pastry cook and laundress who directed many of the domestic operations at Monticello. Their son George Jr. managed the Mulberry Row nailery, while Bagwell Granger was a farm laborer and Isaac a tinsmith and blacksmith. The recollections of Isaac, who also used the surname Jefferson after he became free, were recorded in 1847.

Isaac Granger Jefferson, born in slavery at Monticello in 1775, worked as a nail maker and blacksmith. He also briefly operated a Mulberry Row tin shop, following training in tinsmithing in Philadelphia. After gaining his freedom in the 1820s, he moved to Petersburg, Virginia, where he was photographed, still practicing his blacksmithing trade, at the age of seventy-two.

Despite lifelong efforts to make his operations more efficient and productive, as well as imaginative enterprises like the nailery and millworks, intended to provide additional financial support, Jefferson seldom made a profit from his plantation. His long career in public service prevented full attention to his personal affairs, while international wars and national crises affected the market price of his staple crops. Finally, a severe agricultural depression after 1818 accelerated

OPPOSITE • This tin cup was found during archaeological excavations along Mulberry Row and possibly was made by Isaac Granger Jefferson.

ABOVE • Archaeological evidence suggests that Isaac Granger Jefferson made tinwares in the circa 1793 Storehouse for Iron, reconstructed in the Mountaintop Project. Later the building was used for enslaved worker housing and nail making. During peak production, enslaved boys—aged ten to sixteen—made eight to ten thousand nails a day on Mulberry Row.

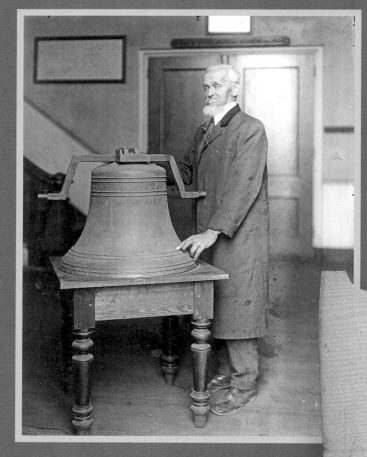

ABOVE · Henry Martin, who for many years rang the bell in the Rotunda of the University of Virginia, recalled that he was born at Monticello on the day Jefferson died. His enslaved parents worked in the Monticello house.

RIGHT · The ten Monticello slaves who gained their freedom either during Jefferson's lifetime or in his will were all members of the extended Hemings family. At right is Jefferson's deed of manumission granting freedom to Robert Hemings in 1794.

"The whole commerce between master and slave is a perpetual exercise of the most boisterous passions, the most unremitting despotism on the one part, and degrading submissions on the other. Our children see this, and learn to imitate it; for man is an imitative animal."

—Thomas Jefferson

This indenture witnesseth that I Thomas Jefferson of county of Albemarle have manumitted and made free Robert Hemings, son of Betty Hemmings: so that in fu he shall be free & of free condition, with all his goods & and shall be discharged of all obligation of bondage or se whatsoever: and that neither myself, my heirs executors o -trators shall have any right to exact from him herea services or duties whatsoever. in witness whereof I have seal to this present deed of manumission. Given in a this twenty fourth day of December one thousand and ninety four.

Signed, sealed and delivered in presence of
D. Carr.

Th Jefferson

a deepening cycle of debt. Jefferson died in 1826 owing over $100,000. His furnishings, books and paintings, farm equipment, the people he owned, and finally his house and lands were sold off to help pay the immense debt.

Jefferson freed only seven enslaved men in his lifetime and in his will; three other slaves were allowed to run away without pursuit. He had often expressed concern for improving the living conditions of his own slaves. The food, clothing, and housing he provided, although inadequate by today's standards, were considered better than the usual plantation provisions. Although Jefferson tried to mitigate slavery's violence, his frequent absences from Monticello meant that many of his slaves were subjected to whippings and other forms of cruelty at the hands of the white overseers. Having, as he said, "scruples about selling negroes but for delinquency, or on their own request," Jefferson only reluctantly bought or sold slaves.[12] Economic difficulties, however, forced him to sell over 120 slaves during his lifetime, and his death left the remainder unprotected from sale and separation.

At his death, men, women, and children accounted for 90 percent of the appraised value of Jefferson's Albemarle County farms (excluding land and furnishings).

EXECUTOR'S SALE.

WILL be sold on the premises, on the first day of January, 1827, that well known and valuable estate called Poplar Forest, lying in the counties of Bedford and Campbell, the property of Thomas Jefferson, dec. within eight miles of Lynchburg and three of New London; also about 70 likely and valuable negroes, with stock, crops, &c. The terms of sale will be accommodating and made known previous to the day.

On the fifteenth of January, at Monticello, in the county of Albemarle; the whole of the residue of the personal property of Thomas Jefferson, dec., consisting of 130 valuable negroes, stock, crop, &c. household and kitchen furniture. The attention of the public is earnestly invited to this property. The negroes are believed to be the most valuable for their number ever offered at one time in the State of Virginia. The household furniture, many valuable historical and portrait paintings, busts of marble and plaister of distinguished individuals; one of marble of Thomas Jefferson, by Caracci, with the pedestal and truncated column on which it stands; a polygraph or copying instrument used by Thomas Jefferson, for the last twenty-five years; with various other articles curious and useful to men of business and private families. The terms of sale will be accommodating and made known previous to the day. The sales will be continued from day to day until completed. These sales being unavoidable, it is a sufficient guarantee to the public, that they will take place at the times and places appointed.

THOMAS J. RANDOLPH,

Nov. 3.   51—tds   Executor of Th. Jefferson, dec.

The 130 men, women, and children living in slavery at Monticello accounted for 90 percent of the appraised value of Jefferson's Albemarle County farms at his death. They were sold along with household furniture, books, paintings, farm equipment, and eventually the house itself, with the proceeds applied toward his debts of $100,000.

The Hemings Family

Elizabeth Hemings (1735–1807), the daughter of a slave ship captain and an African woman, was the matriarch of the largest family at Monticello, numbering nearly eighty people spanning five generations. She belonged to Jefferson's father-in-law, John Wayles, who fathered six of her twelve children, making them half siblings of his wife, Martha. Jefferson inherited the Hemings family upon the death of Wayles in 1773.

The Hemings family enjoyed favored status at Monticello with most of them working as craftsmen or house servants. John Hemmings (his spelling) was a woodworker. Robert Hemings, his brother Martin, and their nephew Burwell served as butlers and personal servants to Jefferson. Wormley Hughes was the head gardener and cared for the horses. Elizabeth Hemings's daughters, Critta and Sally Hemings, performed light work in the house and served as lady's maids.

James Hemings (1765–1801) was a chef de cuisine, trained in Paris, yet he was born into slavery and lived much of his life enslaved. At thirty years of age, he negotiated with Jefferson for legal manumission. According to this agreement, Hemings would be manumitted after training another slave to take his place as chief cook in the Monticello kitchen. James trained his younger brother, Peter, in the original kitchen located under the South Pavilion from 1794 to 1796. After beginning his life as a free man, Hemings traveled and pursued his career as a chef, but unfortunately his career and life in freedom ended abruptly at the age of thirty-six, the result of a possible suicide.

Of the more than 600 individuals Jefferson owned through his lifetime, he freed only ten, all members of the Hemings family, including his mixed-race children with Sally Hemings.

ABOVE • According to oral history, on her deathbed, Martha Jefferson gave this bell to her half sister Sally Hemings.

Peter Hemings was the first resident of the Cook's Room (ABOVE) adjacent to the Kitchen. He had become head cook on the departure, in 1796, of his freed brother James, who penned this inventory of the Monticello Kitchen (RIGHT). In 1809, one of the two cooks trained in French cookery in the President's House in Washington, Edith Fossett or Fanny Hern, moved into this space.

Inventory of Kitchen Utincils

19 Copper Stew pans — 19 Covers
6 Small Sauce pans
3 Copper Baking Moulds
2 Small preserving pans
2 Large ——— Ditto
2 Copper Fish kettles
2 Copper Brazing pans
2 Round Large ——— Ditto
2 Iron Stew pans
2 Large Boiling kettles tin'd inside
1 Large Brass ——— Ditto
12 pewter water Dishes
12 ——— ——— plates
3 Tin Coffee pots
8 Tin Dish Covers
2 hving hangs of Iron & one of [...]

Elizabeth-Ann Isaacs (ABOVE LEFT) and her brother Peter Fossett (ABOVE RIGHT) were Elizabeth Hemings's great-grandchildren, born in slavery at Monticello to Joseph and Edith Fossett, the head blacksmith and head cook. Peter Fossett became, in freedom, a prominent Baptist minister in Ohio.

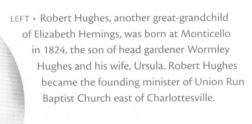

LEFT · Robert Hughes, another great-grandchild of Elizabeth Hemings, was born at Monticello in 1824, the son of head gardener Wormley Hughes and his wife, Ursula. Robert Hughes became the founding minister of Union Run Baptist Church east of Charlottesville.

ABOVE · Many members of the Hemings family passed back and forth along the underground passageway, which linked the domestic activities of the Kitchen, Smokehouse, Washhouse, and storerooms with the main house.

LEFT · John Wayles Jefferson (1835–92), the oldest child of Eston Hemings and Julia Isaacs Jefferson, was a Union Army officer, hotelkeeper, and cotton merchant.

RIGHT · Eston Hemings's son, Beverly Frederick Hemings (grandson of Sally Hemings and Thomas Jefferson), is pictured on the left with three of his sons, circa 1900. No images of Sally Hemings or her children are known.

The Hemings Family

Sally Hemings

Sally Hemings (1773–1835) is one of the most famous—and least understood— African American women in U.S. history. For more than 200 years, her name has been linked to Thomas Jefferson as his enslaved "concubine," obscuring the facts of her life and her identity. While sexual encounters between masters and slaves were common, their connection was exploited by Jefferson's political enemies to discredit him.

Hemings came to Monticello as inherited property with her mother and siblings after the death of her father, John Wayles. Wayles was also father to Jefferson's wife, Martha Wayles Skelton, making Sally Hemings her younger half sister. From a young age, Sally Hemings was a nursemaid to Jefferson's younger daughter Maria and in 1787, when Hemings was 14, she went with her to France. Here she joined her brother James Hemings, who was in training as a chef, while she served as a lady's maid to Jefferson's two daughters. Her son, Madison Hemings, recounted that in Paris his mother became "Mr. Jefferson's concubine." Yet in France, slaves were legally free, and when the family began plans to return to Virginia, Sally Hemings negotiated and received "a solemn pledge that her children should be freed at the age of twenty-one," and Jefferson "promised her extraordinary privileges" if she would return with him to Monticello.

Like countless enslaved women, Sally Hemings bore children fathered by her owner. She herself was the child of an enslaved woman and her owner, as were five of her siblings. Female slaves had no legal right to refuse the sexual advances of the men who owned them.

Unlike countless enslaved women, Sally Hemings was able to negotiate with her owner. The agreement she made with Jefferson in Paris allowed "extraordinary privileges" for herself and freedom for her unborn children. Sally Hemings was exempted from hard labor and instead charged with caring for Jefferson's chamber and wardrobe and sewing. Over the next thirty-two years Hemings raised four children and prepared them for their eventual emancipation. She did not negotiate for, or ever receive, legal freedom in Virginia.

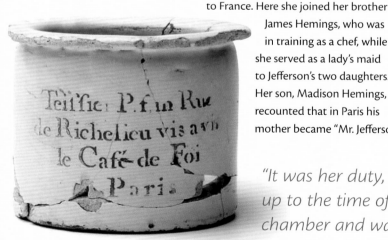

RIGHT • The French ointment pot, found in excavations below Mulberry Row, may have been brought back from Paris by James or Sally Hemings.

"It was her duty, all her life which I can remember, up to the time of father's death, to take care of his chamber and wardrobe, look after us children and do such light work as sewing."

—Madison Hemings, *Pike County (Ohio) Republican*, 1873
Son of Sally Hemings and Thomas Jefferson

Sally Hemings left no written accounts, a common consequence of enslavement. Jefferson's plantation records and her son Madison Hemings's reminiscences are the most important written sources about her life. Though no known portraits exist, fellow slave Isaac Granger Jefferson described her as "very handsome."

Sally Hemings had at least six children fathered by Jefferson. Four survived to adulthood: a daughter, Harriet, and three sons, Beverly, Madison, and Eston. Jefferson delivered on his promise made in Paris. Harriet and Beverly were allowed to leave Monticello after turning twenty-one, and Madison and Eston were freed through a provision in his will. Sally Hemings was never legally emancipated. Instead, she was unofficially freed—or "given her time"—by Jefferson's daughter after his death in 1826. Madison Hemings reported that his mother lived in Charlottesville with him and his brother Eston until her death in 1835. The location of her grave is unknown.

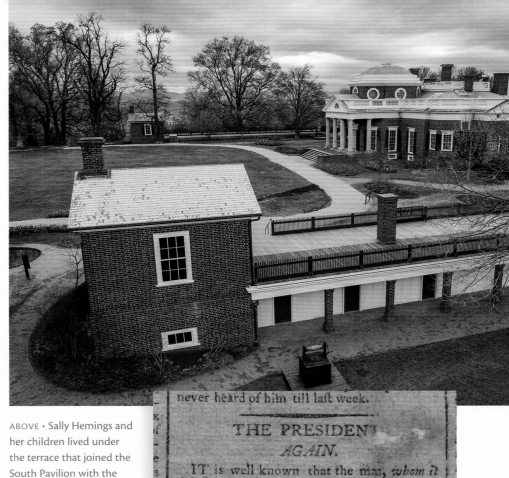

ABOVE • Sally Hemings and her children lived under the terrace that joined the South Pavilion with the house. Their 14' × 15' room was one of two reserved in the South Wing for those working in the house.

ABOVE • In 1802, journalist James Callender accused Thomas Jefferson of having children with an enslaved woman named Sally. His article was the first public acknowledgement of Sally Hemings.

ABOVE • *Elevation of L'Hôtel de Langeac* by Jean-F.T. Chalgrin, 1773. Sally and James Hemings lived in the Hôtel de Langeac, Jefferson's primary residence in Paris.

"Though enslaved, Sally Hemings helped shape her life and the lives of her children, who got an almost 50-year head start on emancipation, escaping the system that had engulfed their ancestors and millions of others. Whatever we may feel about it today, this was important to her."

—Pulitzer Prize–winning historian Annette Gordon-Reed, 2017

Mulberry Row

The center of plantation operations at Monticello was a 1,300-foot road called Mulberry Row, named for the trees that lined it. This was the principal plantation street that served as the dynamic, industrial hub of Jefferson's 5,000-acre enterprise. It was the center of work and domestic life for dozens of enslaved people, free blacks, and free and indentured white workmen.

The work along Mulberry Row contributed to Jefferson's major goals of economy and efficiency in plantation operations. He had his enslaved laborers trained in a wide variety of skills, experimented with the most up-to-date labor-saving machinery, and inaugurated several enterprises to supplement the income from sales of annual crops of tobacco and wheat.

Mulberry Row changed dramatically over time. Structures were built, removed, and repurposed as workers were assigned to different tasks and trades to accommodate Jefferson's changing plans. At the height of activity, circa 1797, there were more than twenty-two workshops, storage buildings, and dwellings. The stable stood at its northeast terminus with sheds for storing charcoal at the southwest end. Between were five log dwellings for slaves, a stone house for free resident workmen that later served as a textile workshop for weaving, a washhouse, a smokehouse and dairy, a blacksmith shop and nailery, a saw pit, a necessary, and two woodworking shops.

ABOVE • In 1796, there were five single-family log dwellings on Mulberry Row, ranging in size from twelve by fourteen feet to fourteen by seventeen feet.

RIGHT • Costumed interpreters (LEFT TO RIGHT) Dylan Pritchett, Marion Dobbins, and Robert Watson on Mulberry Row.

In the nailmaking shop, enslaved boys aged ten to twenty began to produce eight to ten thousand nails a day in 1794. Production was interrupted during the War of 1812 with the difficulty of obtaining nailrod. Production resumed in 1815 at another shop built off Mulberry Row, but it never reached the prewar capacity.

Textile operations were prompted by the embargo of 1808–9 and then the War of 1812 that curtailed imported cloth. Jefferson's goal was to expand his textile operations and provide the cloth needed for Monticello's enslaved families. He experimented with

spinning machines, looms, and carding machines. From 1813 women and girls in the mechanized textile workshop on Mulberry Row made two thousand yards of cloth a year.

In addition to the trades, Mulberry Row included dwellings for some of the slaves who maintained Jefferson's household as seamstresses, chambermaids, parlor maids, valets, cooks, wet nurses, and laundresses. With their services so frequently needed, they were kept close to the main house. The bustling plantation hub during the day became a neighborhood at night for key slaves living there.

Descendants of Monticello's enslaved families plant a new mulberry tree on Mulberry Row in celebration of the completion of the first phase of the Mountaintop Project, May 2, 2015.

Jefferson's Stable

"From breakfast, or noon at latest, to dinner, I am mostly on horseback, attending to my farms or other concerns, which I find healthful to my body, mind, & affairs."

—Thomas Jefferson

Jefferson owned dozens of riding and carriage horses. As Edmund Bacon, a Monticello overseer, once noted, Jefferson was "passionately fond of a good horse." Describing the horse as the "most sovereign of all Doctors," Jefferson took daily rides across his 5,000-acre plantation for exercise and to oversee the work of around 130 enslaved men, women and children.

Enslaved grooms cared for Jefferson's valuable blooded stock, preparing the horses for riding or pulling a carriage. From 1809 until 1826, the chief groom was enslaved hostler Wormley Hughes. Jefferson described him as "one of the most trusty servants I have." He was responsible for the horses in the stable on Mulberry Row and prepared Jefferson's

horse for his daily ride. He also kept the tack clean, maintained the carriages, and supervised younger enslaved men who fed and watered the horses. Biographer Henry Randall remarked on Hughes's passion for horses in 1851: "He could distinctly remember, and describe the points, height, color, pace, temper, etc. of every horse."

Jefferson kept his most prized horses in stables built on Mulberry Row. From 1808 through 1809 he replaced a circa 1793 log stable with a more permanent L-shaped building consisting of two stone bays with a long rear addition. The stone bays were likely used to store feed and tack, while Jefferson's riding and carriage horses were housed in the addition.

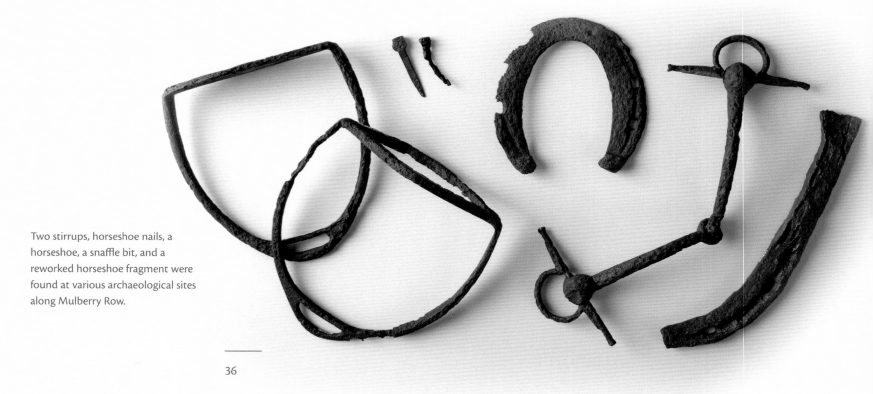

Two stirrups, horseshoe nails, a horseshoe, a snaffle bit, and a reworked horseshoe fragment were found at various archaeological sites along Mulberry Row.

DIOMED.

BY FLORIZEL — A DAUGHTER OF SPECTATOR — GRANDSON OF KING HEROD & GREATGRANDSON OF THE GODOLPHIN BARB
Owned by Sir Charles Bunbury — Trained by Robert Saunders — Ridden by Sam Arnull.
Winner of the First Derby Stakes at Epsom 1780 and other races.
He was sold to Colonel John Hoomes of Virginia U.S.A. for 1000 guineas in 1798 and became The Father of the American Turf.
He was the sire of Grey Diomed Young Diomed, Sir Archy & many others. He died in 1808.
From the original picture by George Stubbs R.A.

In 1808, Jefferson began rebuilding his log stable at the northeast end of
Mulberry Row in stone. Completed in 1809, it was restored in 2016 as part
of the Mountaintop Project. Here, Wormley Hughes looked after Jefferson's
carriage and saddle horses—Bremo, Diomede, Tecumseh, Wellington, and Eagle.
Imported English thoroughbred racing champions such as Diomed (LEFT) were
prized in early Virginia; Jefferson's Diomede was a son from Diomed.

The first *Getting Word* interview in 1993 was with George (Jack) Pettiford (1926–96), a direct descendant of Madison Hemings. His wife, Jacqueline Diggs Pettiford (ABOVE), with some of their children and grandchildren on the west lawn at Monticello.

Getting Word

"Then began our troubles. We were scattered all over the country, never to meet each other again until we meet in another world." Peter Fossett, former enslaved house servant at Monticello, recalled the peril brought upon the African American families of Monticello after Jefferson's death. Fossett's interview was with the *New York World* of Cincinnati in 1898. Almost one hundred years later, during the bicentennial celebration commemorating the two hundredth anniversary of Thomas Jefferson's birth, Monticello historians Lucia "Cinder" Stanton and Dianne Swann-Wright, along with project consultant Beverly Gray, began the *Getting Word* Oral History Project. These pioneering women logged over forty thousand travel miles and countless hours traversing territory in fourteen states while seeking out descendants of the Hern, Hemings, Fossett, Granger, Gillette, and other African American families of Monticello. A connection with descendants of Brown Colbert in Liberia made *Getting Word* an international endeavor. What began as a project to document how enslaved people experienced slavery at Monticello has evolved into a critically important tool for expressing the full breadth of African American history in America. *Getting Word* has revealed that descendants of African American families at Monticello played important roles in the Civil War, Niagara Movement, Student Non-Violent Coordinating Committee, and the continued struggle to realize the

Descendants of Monticello's enslaved families gathered on the East Portico steps before the National Endowment for the Humanities Summit on "Memories, Mourning, and Mobilization: Legacies of Slavery and Freedom in America," held at Monticello in 2016.

enduring promise of Jefferson's words that "all men are created equal."

Since the project's inception, more than two hundred people have recounted their family traditions and stories for historians. *Getting Word* has now become one of the most sustained oral history archives dedicated to the experience of slavery and its legacies. In 2012, *Getting Word* began receiving national attention and exposure with the exhibition "Slavery at Jefferson's Monticello: Paradox of Liberty," co-organized with the Smithsonian's National Museum of African American History and Culture. The exhibit has continued to travel

to museums around the country, reaching an audience of over one million Americans. The project also received national exposure from NBC's *Today* show and participation in the Slave Dwelling Project, as well as through events held at Monticello.

Families who participated during the early years of the project are now returning with their children and grandchildren. *Getting Word* reconnects families and provides a vehicle for descendants of the Monticello diaspora to see each other again "in this world." The project and descendants of Monticello's enslaved community continue to thrive.

Thomas Jefferson's
ESSAY IN
Architecture

BY WILLIAM L. BEISWANGER

Robert H. Smith Director Emeritus of Restoration at Monticello

In March 1809, Thomas Jefferson was at long last liberated from what he called the "splendid misery"[1] of the presidency of the United States, free to begin the evening of his life in retirement at Monticello. The event coincided with the essential completion of a house he had begun more than forty years earlier and transformed, beginning in 1796, from an eight-room to a twenty-one-room dwelling. The finish joinery, plastering, and painting alone took more than ten years of steady work to complete. What Jefferson created—for he was indeed its architect—was unlike any other house in the United States, and not just because it was the first house in this country to have a dome. It was unusual in both plan and elevation. Jefferson himself acknowledged that it ranked "among the curiosities of the neighborhood,"[2] and apart from its setting, which few could fault, apparently many who saw the house found it too idiosyncratic to be pleasing or even comprehensible. One visitor, some thirteen years after Jefferson's death, called it "a monument of ingenious extravagance without unity or uniformity, upon which architecture seem[s] to have exerted, if not exhausted, the versatility of her genius." The critic went on to state: "We will venture to say that Mr. Jefferson had no distinct conception of any design when he commenced building, but enlarged, added and modified as his ingenuity contrived, until this incomprehensible pile reached this acme of its destiny in which it stands at present, still indeed unfinished."[3] It is true that Monticello lacks the purity and geometric simplicity of Jefferson's other buildings, such as the Rotunda at the University of Virginia or Poplar Forest, his octagonal retreat in Bedford County, Virginia. By contrast, Monticello showed all the signs of a modified and evolving plan, which is

Jefferson's freehand drawing of Monticello shows the north and south bows that were added to the house circa 1777. The sketch could date from his years in Paris (1784–89), when he began thinking about enlarging the house. On the verso is a plan for adding two first-floor rooms.

perhaps why he called it his "essay in architecture."[4]

He began the essay in 1768 at the age of twenty-five, the year he contracted with a Mr. Moore to level an area 250 feet square at the northeast end of the mountaintop.[5] It is clear from Jefferson's surviving drawings and notes that even in this early period he served as his own architect. In this art he was self-taught, gaining knowledge and inspiration from books and close observation. Monticello was, as far as we

The Marquis de Chastellux, who visited Monticello in 1782, said that the house "resembled none of the others seen in this country," and that Thomas Jefferson was "the first American who has consulted the Fine Arts to know how he should shelter himself from the weather." Jefferson's drawing of the house from the early 1770s reflects his rejection of the architectural tradition in Virginia and his interest in a stricter application of classical form as he understood it from the published works of the sixteenth-century architect and theorist Andrea Palladio.

know, the first of his many architectural projects and, as it turns out, the most richly documented. Of the more than seven hundred architectural drawings and notes in Jefferson's hand, nearly half relate to the house and plantation at Monticello.[6]

For the most part, Jefferson rejected the architectural tradition established in Virginia. Compared even to dwellings elsewhere in the American colonies at that time, his drawing of the elevation of the house reveals a stricter—almost academic—application of classical sources and the Roman architectural orders. In one sense the facade of the first Monticello was a mathematical exercise in the use of the classical orders, and in this regard the young architect was guided principally by Andrea Palladio and his *Four Books of Architecture*, first published in 1570.[7] When the Marquis de Chastellux saw the house under construction in 1782, he went so far as to announce its uniqueness to the world, stating unequivocally that it "resembled none of the others seen in this country."[8]

Jefferson began by first constructing a rather modest six-room house. On the first floor was a parlor flanked by a chamber and a dining room, and on the second level, two bedrooms and a lofty study to house his growing library. It was about 1776 that Jefferson's propensity for alteration first surfaced in a significant way. He modified the already existing West (garden) Front by adding a two-story canted bay projection to the parlor and study, and added one-story rooms, also of a partial octagonal shape, to the dining room and chamber. During the period of the 1770s he also devised a scheme for linking an impressive array of support rooms to the cellars of the house by L-shaped wings

Although the scheme for the L-shaped terraces that link the pavilions to the house dates from the 1770s, it was not executed until after 1800, and then only in modified form. This terrace landscape is perhaps the most universally satisfying aspect of Jefferson's design for Monticello.

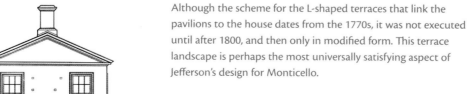

concealed in the hillside. This scheme, however, was not constructed until after 1800, and
then only in a modified and greatly curtailed
form. But it was this eight-room house and the
plans for its completion, including ideas for
decorating some of the rooms "entirely in the
antique style," that impressed the Marquis de
Chastellux, and prompted the remarkable com-
ment that Jefferson was "the first American who has consulted the Fine
Arts to know how he should shelter himself from the weather."[9]

Plan of the first floor of
Monticello as remodeled,
beginning in 1796, and
completed by 1809. The
superimposed plan of the
earlier house is indicated
in blue.

The shell of the house was basically completed—certainly hab-
itable—by 1784, when Jefferson departed for France on what would
become a five-year diplomatic mission. The evidence suggests, however, that he had
not completed—perhaps not even begun—the interior finish work, such as the moldings and plastering. This might explain his comment to George Wythe in 1794 that he
was "living in a brick-kiln ... my house, in it's [sic] present state, is nothing better."[10]

While living in Paris, he experienced firsthand a new level of refinement in
domestic architecture. The elegant town house that he rented on the corner of the
Champs-Élysées and the rue de Berri had modern conveniences such as flush toilets
and skylights that transformed spaces with diffused light.[11] There
were the requisite formal "rooms of entertainment" and also a variety of private and intimate spaces that greatly
enhanced comfort and convenience. The
grouping of these spaces to form what could
be called apartments was particularly an eye-
opener for Jefferson. By contrast, the plan of the

In 1796, acting on a new plan, Jefferson began a dramatic transformation of Monticello. The upper story was removed, the East Front (ABOVE) extended, and a new second level created within the height of the original first floor. The appearance suggests a one-story house.

OPPOSITE • The dome, constructed in 1800, was the first on a house in America. Jefferson based the proportions on the ancient Temple of Vesta in Rome. Although the portico and the dome are the central feature of the West (garden) Front, the unifying elements are the entablature and balustrade carried around the perimeter of the building.

The East Portico frames a recessed arcaded wall. The piers between the doors and windows are actually wood over brick, sand-painted in imitation of finely tooled sandstone. The stone columns date from the early house and were reused when the house was enlarged in 1796.

house he left behind in Virginia must have seemed formal and stiff.

In 1796, acting on a new plan, Jefferson began a dramatic transformation of Monticello. The upper story was removed, the East Front extended, and a new second level created for bedrooms within the height of the first floor. He referred to the new upper rooms as the "Mezzaninos."[12] The square windows for this mezzanine level are compressed between the main entablature and the cornice of the window below. Inside, the sills are only seven inches above the floor. On the third floor, three additional bedrooms are concealed in the northeast attic and lighted by skylights. The overall exterior appearance suggests a one-story house—an idea consistent with the progressive French thinking on domestic architecture so much admired by Jefferson.

For the West Front, he lowered the height of the second-floor study by eight feet and over it constructed a dome inspired by the Temple of Vesta at Rome illustrated in Giacomo Leoni's handsome edition of Palladio's *Four Books of Architecture*. By necessity, Jefferson had to adapt the circular form to an octagonal plan, but the proportions of the dome (one-third of a circle) and the rise and projection of the three steps at its base were preserved."[13]

The Doric portico and dome are the central focus of the facade, but the unifying horizontal elements of this neoclassical essay are the Doric entablature and balustrade carried around the perimeter of the building. Jefferson's use, however, of a Chinese lattice railing on top of the house seems to challenge the hierarchy if not the primacy of the classical orders.

Glass doors and triple-sash windows, which also serve as doorways, connect the spacious Hall to the East Portico. The linkage of these two spaces is further suggested by the floor and glossy floorcloth, both painted grass green at the suggestion of the portrait painter Gilbert Stuart.

Jefferson's plan called for retaining the rooms on the main floor that ranged along the West Front and for advancing the East Front to accommodate a large entrance hall/museum, a library, and three bedrooms. The old and new spaces in the wings were to be organized around lateral passageways off the Hall. He rejected the idea of a great staircase in the Hall and instead provided a much smaller one in each of the passageways. He reasoned that "great staircases ... are expensive & occupy a space which would make a good room in every story."[14] But it was also consistent with his view that the merely ceremonial should be avoided. Jefferson's apartment occupied most of the south end of the house while two guest bedrooms were on the north side. The chamber on the south side was used as a family sitting room and schoolroom, although it has an alcove for a bed, as do the two guest chambers. Jefferson summarized his approach for reorganizing the house in a letter to John Brown in 1797: "In Paris particularly all the new & good houses are of a single story, that is of the height of 16. or 18. f. generally, & the whole of it given to the rooms of entertainment; but in the parts where there are bedrooms they have two tiers of them of from 8. to 10. f. high each, with a small private staircase."[15] In following the logic of the French parti, Jefferson created an asymmetrical distribution of high-ceilinged rooms for the main floor. The result was the irregular plan of the second level. Four chambers, each with bed alcoves, ranged along the East Front. Over the Cabinet was the room Jefferson called the "Appendix," and next to it the Nursery (for grandchildren) tucked into the low-ceilinged room above the Greenhouse.[16] The cantilevered gallery in the Hall connected the north and south spaces.

Jefferson's asymmetrical distribution of high-ceilinged rooms for the main floor resulted in the irregular plan of the second level. This asymmetry is not evident, however, when one views the West (garden) Front.

It is remarkable that Jefferson, a widower since 1782, would see a need to more than double the size of his house. When he began the enterprise he wrote a friend, "I am uncovering & repairing my house, which during my absence had gone much to decay." However, he went on to explain, "I make some alterations in it with a greater eye to convenience than I had when younger."[17] Convenience, one could argue, was largely self-centered. Even so, when his family joined him in 1809, the house apparently functioned well. In that first year of his retirement there were living at Monticello his eldest daughter, Martha, her husband, Thomas Mann Randolph, and six of the eight Randolph children, ages ranging from eight months to twelve years. In time three additional children would be born, and Jefferson's sister Anne Scott Jefferson Marks would join this domestic scene. His apartment, for indeed it could he called that, occupied the width of the southeast side of the house and about one-third the length of the long West (garden) Front. At its core were the Bed Chamber, Cabinet (study), and Library. Although the first two rooms existed in modified form in the pre-1796 house, the Library was an addition. Its incorporation into the apartment marked a significant change from the earlier version of Monticello, where the library above the parlor was probably the second most impressive architectural space in the house. Its elimination when Jefferson decided to spread out all his principal rooms on the ground floor shows how far he had come to value convenience over ceremony and architectural display.

A bed alcove was first planned where the elliptical arch is now. But Jefferson changed his mind and decided to extend his Cabinet and Library the full width of the building. Margaret Bayard Smith found the "numerous divisions & arches" in Jefferson's apartment disappointing, and thought that one large room would have been more impressive.

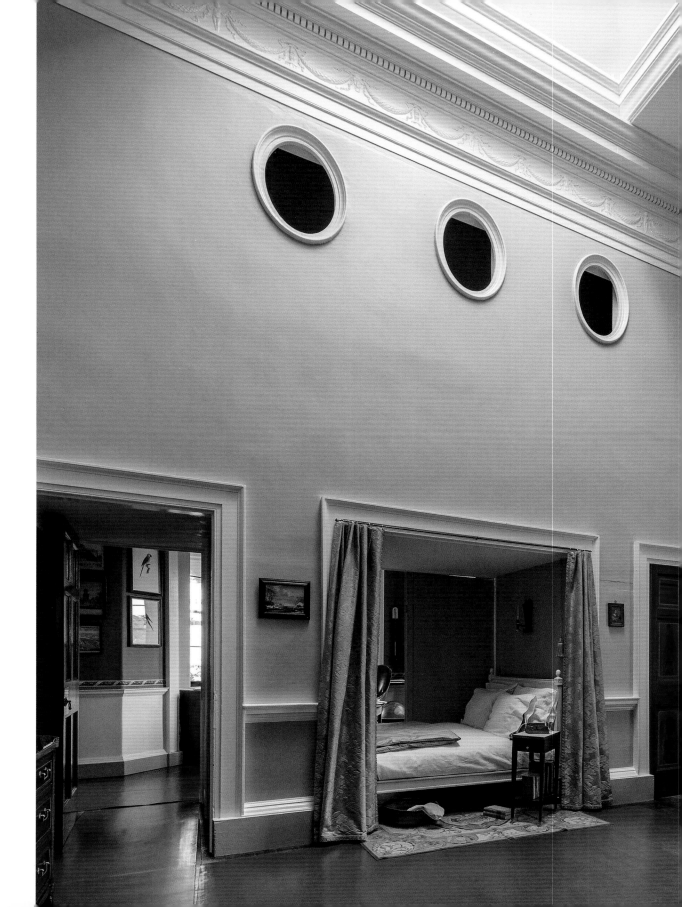

The nearly 19-foot-high Bed Chamber is lighted by a skylight and triple-sash window. Above the bed alcove is a closet vented and illuminated by three elliptical openings and reached by a ladder in the closet (RIGHT).

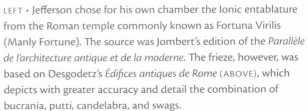

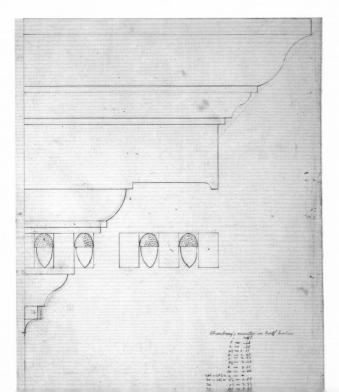

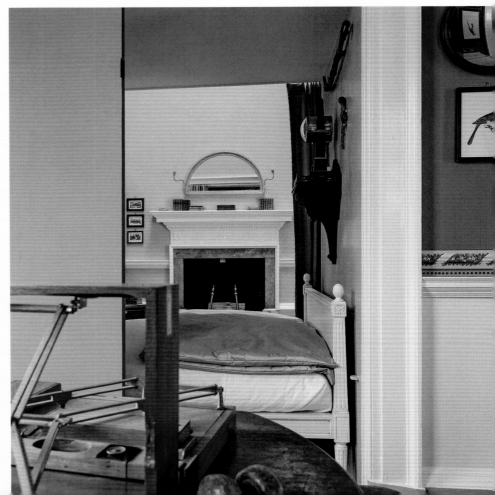

Glass doors lead from the Library to the South Piazza (also called the Greenhouse), another space in Jefferson's apartment.

Jefferson's suite is L-shaped and the spaces are connected in such a way that one hesitates to call them three separate rooms. Besides conventional doorways, features such as a bed in an alcove open on both sides, and arches—one broad and elliptical and the other narrow and semicircular—are employed as transitions from one space to another. Variety is introduced by changes in ceiling heights and in the amount and quality of natural light admitted. The Bed Chamber, for example, is nearly nineteen feet high and flooded with light from a large skylight and a triple-sash window. To moderate the light and heat in summer, Jefferson designed a louvered blind with movable slats to close over the skylight.

In his scheme, he stated, "my blinds open back on hinges as in the winter we want both the light and warmth of the sun."[18] The two other spaces in Jefferson's suite (above which are the family bedrooms on the second floor) are ten feet high and lighted by more conventional windows and sash doors.

The irregular layout of the apartment was noteworthy for its time in a country where symmetry and balance were so highly esteemed. Margaret Bayard Smith, who was otherwise an ardent admirer of Jefferson, sided with the critics, confessing, "I own I was much disappointed in its appearance, & I do not think with its numerous divisions & arches it is as impressive as one large room would have been."[19]

Mrs. Smith referred to the apartment as Jefferson's "sanctum sanctorum."[20] There he spent the morning hours until breakfast, after which he visited his gardens or rode off to inspect his plantation. His granddaughter Ellen Wayles Randolph Coolidge remembered:

As the day, in summer, grew warmer he retired to his own apartments. ... Here he remained until about one o'clock, occupied in reading, writing, looking over papers, etc. My mother would sometimes send me with a message to him. A gentle knock, a call of "come in." and I would enter, with a mixed feeling of love and reverence, and some pride in being the bearer of a communication.[21]

Perhaps the most remarkable feature of the apartment was the integration of three outdoor rooms that added greatly to Jefferson's comfort, convenience, and

In writing to William Hamilton on March 1, 1808, Jefferson observed, "My green house is only a piazza adjoining my study, because I mean it for nothing more than some oranges, Mimosa Farnesiana & a very few things of that kind." The piazza was also to house an aviary for Jefferson's pet mockingbirds.

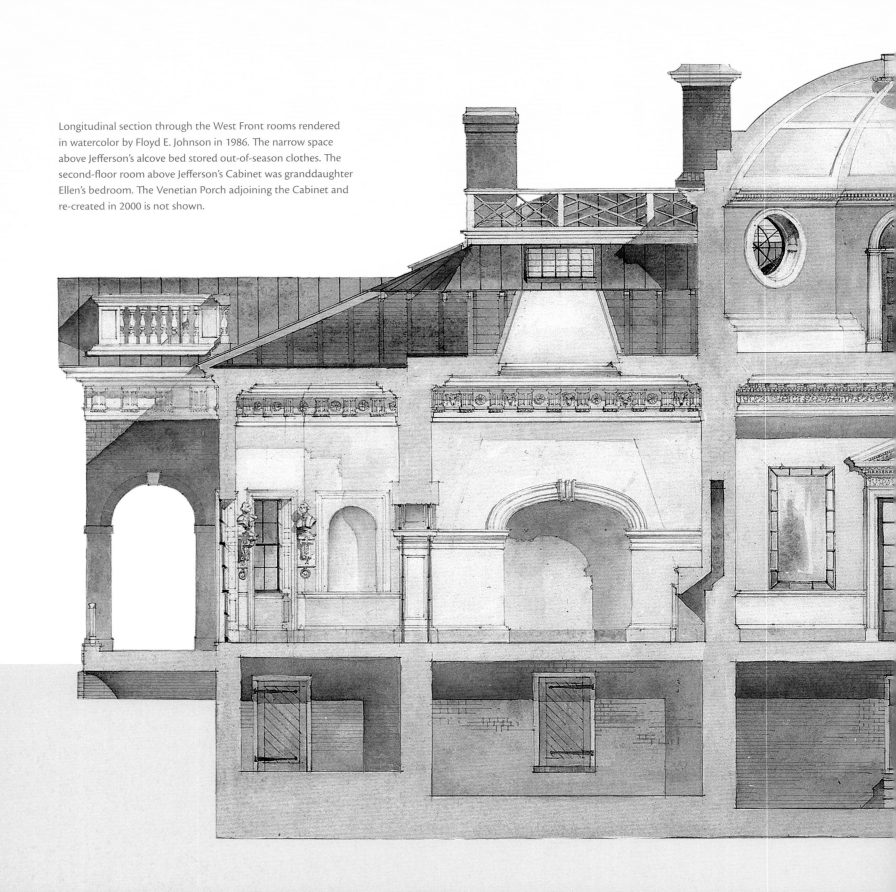

Longitudinal section through the West Front rooms rendered in watercolor by Floyd E. Johnson in 1986. The narrow space above Jefferson's alcove bed stored out-of-season clothes. The second-floor room above Jefferson's Cabinet was granddaughter Ellen's bedroom. The Venetian Porch adjoining the Cabinet and re-created in 2000 is not shown.

Windows that double as doorways appear throughout the first floor of Monticello, including this one leading from the Greenhouse to the Venetian Porch. In this version, the two lower sashes can be raised to the height of a door.

pleasure. Each is basically a porch and each is directly connected to the apartment by folding glass doors. In square footage, the three spaces equal nearly half the area of the Bed Chamber, Cabinet, and Library. Isaac Weld, who was at Monticello the year before the remodeling of 1796 was underway, alluded to at least one of the outdoor spaces when he observed: "A large apartment is laid out for a library and museum, meant to extend the entire breadth of the house, the windows of which are to open into an extensive green house and aviary."[22] The museum was ultimately established in the Hall; the greenhouse and aviary were planned for the arcaded loggia that Jefferson called the South Piazza (Greenhouse), which projects from the center of the southeast facade. This neatly plastered room is nearly twelve feet high and has window sashes on three sides that can be raised to doorway height. Above it on the second floor is a child's nursery. Although there was sufficient light and ventilation, the piazza was apparently not heated, and its success as a greenhouse was limited. However, with the addition of a workbench it functioned admirably as a shop, in which, we are told, Jefferson made models and other small things of wood and metal.[23]

Weld's comment could be interpreted to mean that the aviary was to be a separate room, yet an entry by Jefferson in his building notebook indicates that the piazza was the intended location: "SE. Piazza. from impost to top of architrave an aviary to occupy breadth of recess only."[24] From his note it appears that the floor of the cage was to be aligned with the base of the arched portion of the windows (the imposts)—hence high enough to walk under. The top of the cage was to be level with the top of the window architrave, which in this case is at ceiling height. "Breadth of recess only"

Glass doors connect the Cabinet to the South Venetian Porch. Granddaughter Ellen recalled, "His summer study, where he remained all the morning hours of the fine season, was under a room which was for a long time my own chamber, and, the windows being open, I heard him frequently thus singing the old Psalm tunes, or the Scotch melodies in which in spite of his love for Italian music, he always took great pleasure." Whether the reference is to the Venetian Porch or the Cabinet is uncertain.

The Venetian Porches flanking the South Piazza (Greenhouse) served as cool retreats from the sun. Jefferson could justify them by his belief that design of the house should be "subordinated to the law of convenience." That he struggled to balance convenience and aesthetics is evident in his response to his joiner's query whether there should be a railing on each roof. Jefferson responded, "I do not propose any Chinese railing on the two Porticles at the doors of my Cabinet, because it would make them more conspicuous to the prejudice of the Piazza & it's [*sic*] pediment as the principal object. The intention was that they should be as obscure as possible that they might not disturb the effect of their principal."

is a little more puzzling, but very likely it refers to the back area of the piazza between the side arches and the Library. Although nothing remains of an aviary at Monticello, it is almost certain that somewhere within his apartment he housed his pet mocking-birds. He had three of them in Washington. Margaret Bayard Smith described one:

In the window recesses were stands for the flowers and plants which it was his delight to attend and among his roses and geraniums was suspended the cage of his favorite mocking-bird, which he cherished with peculiar fondness, not only for its melodious powers, but for its uncommon intelligence and affectionate disposition, of which qualities he gave surprising instances. It was the constant companion of his solitary and studious hours. Whenever he was alone he opened the cage and let the bird fly about the room. After flitting for a while from one object to another, it would alight on his table and regale him with its sweetest notes, or perch on his shoulder and take its food from his lips. Often when he retired to his chamber it would hop up the stairs after him and while he took his siesta, would sit on his couch and pour forth its melodious strains.[25]

The birds were shipped to Monticello when Jefferson left Washington in 1809, and on April 25 he was able to send a reassuring word: "My birds arrived here in safety and are the delight of every hour."[26]

Flanking the South Piazza (Greenhouse) are small enclosed terraces that could be entered from the piazza or the adjoining Cabinet or Library, whence one could descend to the lawn. Jefferson sometimes called them "porticles," a word that suggests small porches or porticoes.[27] And he also called them his Venetian Porches—a clear reference to the jalousies (louvered blinds) that constitute the walls.[28] Although they were removed about 1893, they were recorded in early artists' views and photographs, and re-created in 2000 based on those views and Jefferson's plan for the South

The light inside the South Venetian Porch or "porticle" can be modulated by adjusting the angle of the slats in the door blinds or by folding back the double-tier doors in a variety of combinations. One can even remove the lunettes within the arches.

The scheme for uniting the house with L-shaped wings is not unlike examples of villas designed by Andrea Palladio and known to Jefferson from books. The distinction, however, is that the dwelling in a Palladian villa is typically at the head of a courtyard enclosed by the service buildings. But at Monticello Jefferson took advantage of the sloping site and constructed the wings in the hillside, thereby providing access to the service rooms at ground level while preserving uninterrupted views of the landscape from the windows of the house. In short, what he created—unique in American architecture—was a Palladian scheme turned inside out.

Venetian Porch.[29] This plan, which details his scheme for door blinds, probably dates from 1805, when he was ordering similar exterior louvered shutters for the South Piazza (Greenhouse).[30] Within each doorway there were to be two tiers of double bifold blinds with movable slats, each tier four feet high. These were to be the same thickness as the walls: three and one-half inches. The blinds were to be hinged so that when not in use they could swing clear of the arches and fold compactly against the piers. Nowhere does Jefferson mention the function of the Venetian Porches. Privacy might have been a consideration, but more likely they were valued as cool retreats from the sun—a view consistent with his claim that "under the beaming, constant and almost vertical sun of Virginia, shade is our Elysium."[31] It is easy to imagine the pleasure of stepping from the Library or Cabinet into either of these enclosures—perhaps the east one in the morning and the south in the afternoon. The South Venetian Porch might have been, in fact, Jefferson's Summer Study. Ellen. whose room was

above his Cabinet, remembers overhearing her grandfather in his apartment:

Accessible from the Greenhouse, the South Terrace served as an extension of Jefferson's private apartment.

> *His voice continued wonderfully sweet and unbroken even to the last years of his life. He had the habit of singing low or what is called humming in the intervals between his various employments, when he rose from his writing table or reading chair and walked about his rooms. His summer study, where he remained all the morning hours of the fine season, was under a room which was for a long time my own chamber, and, the windows being open, I heard him frequently thus singing the old Psalm tunes, or the Scotch melodies in which in spite of his love for Italian music, he always took great pleasure.[32]*

Regardless of whether the South Venetian Porch or the Cabinet was the Summer Study, Ellen's account reveals her grandfather's habit of seasonal changes within his quarters.

The final component of Jefferson's extended apartment is the raised terrace that leads from the South Piazza (Greenhouse) to a two-story outchamber known as the South Pavilion. A similar terrace arrangement is found on the northwest side of the house. Both terraces are L-shaped, and beneath the nine-foot-wide deck that leads from the piazzas to the angles are passages that link the cellar of the house to wings located under the much broader section of terraces. The scheme is not unlike that of some Palladian villas, where the dwelling is flanked by service buildings forming a U-shaped courtyard. However, at Monticello, Jefferson minimized the sense of courtyard and opened views of the landscape from the house by concealing the wings in the hillside. In short, what he created was a Palladian scheme turned inside out. Although these terraces were not constructed until the first decade of the nineteenth century,

This watercolor, *View of the West Front of Monticello and Garden* by family friend Jane Braddick Peticolas, shows Monticello as it may have appeared in 1825. The scene includes three of Jefferson's Randolph grandchildren: the youngest boy, George Wythe, rolls a hoop, as two of his sisters, Mary and Cornelia, stand together watching. An unidentified young man, seated lower left, sketches the scene.

the initial idea dates from the 1770s and recalls a suggestion made by Lord Kames in his essay "Gardening and Architecture" in the *Elements of Criticism*, a work known to Jefferson by 1771. Kames had proposed an artificial walk elevated high above the plain—an airy walk that would extend and vary the prospect and elevate the mind.[33] From Jefferson's elevated walkway there are views of the gardens and impressive vistas of the plain to the south and east. The design was unique for its time not only in this country but also perhaps in Great Britain and Europe, where terraces connected to buildings were usually raised on much higher platforms. Jefferson's walkways are only about four feet above grade and are more intimately connected to the landscape. The sense is that the main floor of the house extends into the garden. This is perhaps the most universally satisfying aspect of the design of Monticello, and one has only to step from the house onto the wooden terrace and hear the sound of footsteps to experience it. Yet for all its humanism, the image that comes to mind is also patrician, for beneath the walkways, buried in the hillside and therefore out of sight, are the activities of those who labored in his service.

Although Jefferson's apartment best demonstrates the breadth of his thinking about extended living spaces, there are similarly conceived areas on all sides of the house. Projecting from the northwest end of the building is another piazza that outwardly resembles the Greenhouse in its arched openings, exterior entablature, and pediment. However, it is not enclosed with sashes nor is it plastered; it is a true open loggia. The ceiling is also much higher, owing to the absence of a second-floor room.

Embellishing the otherwise stark interior is a Doric entablature based on one from the ancient Roman Baths of Diocletian, where the face of the sun god is repeated in the metopes.

Flanking the piazza are two small terraces with stairs leading to the lawn. Although basically similar to their counterparts on the south side, they were never enclosed. The four corner terraces are probably what Jefferson called the "Angular Portals," for each provides a secondary entry to the house through raised triple-sash windows or French doors. Another feature of each corner terrace is a built-in planting bed that fills the triangular void between the stairs and the canted wall of the house. We are told that violets grew within the triangle outside Jefferson's Cabinet window.[34]

The raised walkway that leads from the North Piazza to the pavilion was known as the "public terrace," which implies that the South Terrace was reserved for the family or perhaps for Jefferson alone.[35] Edmund Bacon, a longtime overseer, recalled, "Mr. Jefferson was always an early riser—arose at daybreak or before. The sun never found him in bed. I used sometimes to think, when I went up there very early in the morning, that I would find him in bed; but there he would be before me, walking on the terrace."[36] Later in the day, according to Ellen, Jefferson would reemerge from his rooms "before sunset to walk on the terrace or the lawn, to see his grandchildren run races, or to converse with his family and friends."[37] So important was this ritual to the aging man that when the snow fell, according to Ellen's sister Virginia, "we would go out, as soon as it stopped, to clear it off the terraces with shovels, that he might have his usual walk on them without treading in snow."[38]

No doubt it was the North Terrace that many had in mind when they mentioned "a favorite promenade in the evening and in damp weather."[39] From here, there are views of the village of Charlottesville, the valley, and the Blue Ridge Mountains

The North Piazza and its entablature are visible from the second-floor North Passage window. Outwardly, the piazza resembles the Greenhouse in its arched openings, exterior entablature, and pediment. Within, it is a very different space: it is a true open loggia with a much higher ceiling owing to the absence of a second-floor room. The only embellishment to this stark brick interior is the massive Doric entablature based on an example from the ancient Roman Baths of Diocletian, where the face of the sun god Apollo is repeated in the metopes.

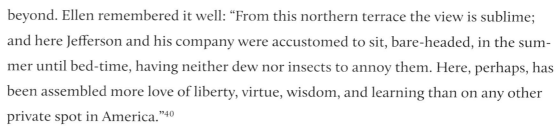

beyond. Ellen remembered it well: "From this northern terrace the view is sublime; and here Jefferson and his company were accustomed to sit, bare-headed, in the summer until bed-time, having neither dew nor insects to annoy them. Here, perhaps, has been assembled more love of liberty, virtue, wisdom, and learning than on any other private spot in America."[40]

Jefferson planned to make the West Portico a more livable space by providing benches and suspending folding louvered blinds between the Doric columns.

The two remaining outdoor rooms at the perimeter of the house are the East Portico (the carriage entrance) adjoining the Hall, and the West Portico adjoining the Parlor and overlooking the flower garden. Jefferson's plan for making these more

livable spaces involved suspending louvered blinds between the Doric columns. The solution was particularly apt for the West Portico, where the afternoon sun is intense. Jefferson considered several schemes, unfortunately none of them dated. The final idea appears to be for two folding blinds suspended between each pair of columns.[41] The lower half can be folded up and secured to the upper half by hooks, or both folded and raised to the ceiling. Nowhere, however, does Jefferson describe the pulley system necessary to raise and lower the blinds, nor has any physical or documentary evidence yet been found to prove that any were installed in either of the porticoes. Furthermore, his mention of "Venetian blinds for the Porticos" in a September 24, 1804, list of work for his slave joiner John Hemmings leaves it unclear whether Jefferson is referring to fabrication or installation.[42]

Four benches, each six feet long, were to furnish the West Portico.[43] Although Jefferson does not specify their placement, one likely plan has two of the benches facing each other along the sides of the portico (between the rear and forward columns) and the other two benches positioned between the front columns and facing the house. This U-shaped arrangement leaves the area between the two middle columns open as a walkway. With the addition of louvered blinds, the portico would have been transformed into an inviting outdoor living room.

Very likely the two eight-foot-long benches planned for the East Portico were to be placed along the open sides of the porch, facing each other as their modern versions do today.[44] But there is also an inventory, taken after Jefferson's death, that lists twenty-eight "black painted [Windsor] chairs" in the adjoining Hall. No doubt many of these were frequently moved outside.[45] Both porticoes are connected to a spacious room by glass doors and triple-sash windows that function as doors. With the sashes raised and the doors open, the two worlds are wonderfully joined. The linkage is further suggested in the Hall by the floor and glossy floorcloth, both painted grass green at the suggestion of Gilbert Stuart.[46] Although it is easy to imagine Jefferson and his family and friends moving freely in and out of doors on a summer evening, we are told that this idyll was frequently marred by the swarms of impertinent gazers who, without introduction, permission, or any ceremony whatever, thrust themselves into the most private of Mr. Jefferson's out-of-door resorts, and even into his house, and stared about as if they were at a public show. When sitting in the shade of his porticoes to enjoy the coolness of the approaching evening, parties of men and women would sometimes approach within a dozen yards, and gaze at him point-blank until they had looked their fill, as they would have gazed on a "lion in a menagerie."[47]

The visitor to Monticello in 1839 quoted previously (p. 42) arrived thirteen years too late to come and gaze at the great man and quiz him about his "monument of ingenious extravagance." Jefferson, who is reputed to have said "Architecture is my delight, and putting up, and pulling down, one of my favorite amusements," was well

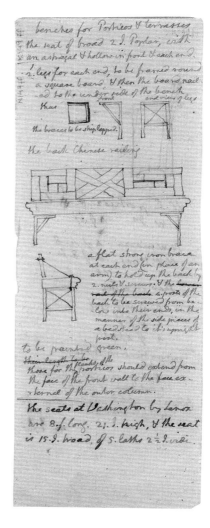

Among Jefferson's designs for furniture is a drawing for Chinese-inspired lattice benches for the "porticoes & terrasses" at Monticello.

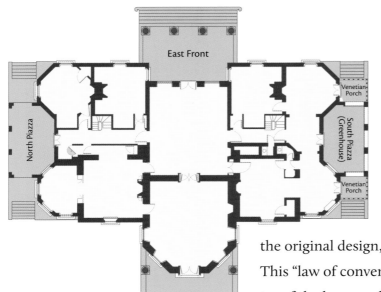

Labels on plan: East Front, Venetian Porch, North Piazza, South Piazza (Greenhouse), Venetian Porch

The green areas summarize the variety of open-air living spaces at the perimeter of the house. By square footage alone, they equal nearly half the area of the first-floor rooms.

aware that what he created was subject to criticism.[48] In the fall of 1809, he wrote to Benjamin Latrobe and invited him to come see his "essay in architecture." Thinking this accomplished architect might accept the offer, he apparently felt obliged to confess that his essay "has been so much subordinated to the law of convenience, & affected also by the circumstance of change in the original design, that it is liable to some unfavorable & just criticisms."[49] This "law of convenience" justifies the open-air living spaces at the perimeter of the house, which, by square footage alone, equal nearly half the area of the main-floor rooms. The fact that each space is slightly different is largely owing to its function and its relationship to the sun and prevailing wind. In breadth and openness the house goes far beyond the typical Virginia plantation dwelling that Jefferson would have known from his youth—houses recognized for their compactness and inward orientation. Monticello embraces the landscape and to a certain degree becomes part of it.

In a sense, at Monticello, Jefferson made permanent the experience of outdoor living that he described during the summer of 1793, when he rented a house on the Schuylkill River to escape from the yellow fever in Philadelphia. With him was his daughter Maria, then enrolled in school, who, Jefferson wrote, "passes two or three days in the week with me, under the trees, for I never go into the house but at the hour of bed. I never before knew the full value of trees. My house is entirely embosomed in high plane trees, with good grass below, & under them I breakfast, dine, write, read and receive my company."[50] Life under the trees ultimately found its venue on the porticoes, piazzas, and terraces of Monticello.

In breadth and openness the house goes far beyond the typical Virginia plantation dwelling that Jefferson would have known from his youth—houses recognized for their compactness and inward orientation. The porticoes, Venetian porches, piazzas, and terraces that comprise the open-air living spaces at the perimeter of the house (visible in part in the photograph to the left) show the extent to which Monticello embraces the landscape and, to a certain degree, becomes part of it.

Decoration
Simple Yet Elegant

Relying primarily on examples from books, Jefferson produced drawings for many of the architectural details at Monticello. They were prepared for his joiners, principally James Dinsmore, assisted by two of Jefferson's slaves, John Hemmings and Lewis.

The joiners were responsible for the finished woodwork and produced all the door casings, the base moldings, chair rails, and entablatures required for each room. The primary exceptions to the use of wood were the frieze ornaments and other fine details, such as the egg and dart, rosettes, and acanthus leaves that were applied to the woodwork. These were made in Washington from a material called composition—a mixture of whiting, linseed oil, hide glue, and rosin, heated and pressed into molds. The exceptions are the sun-god faces made of lead for the North Piazza.

ABOVE • Even excluding most of the sashes, which were made in Philadelphia, and the doors, made in Richmond, the finished woodwork at Monticello took ten years to complete.

Jefferson chose the Roman architectural orders, exhibited in their hierarchy, as the basis of the "simple yet regular and elegant" decorative scheme noted by the Duc de La Rochefoucauld-Liancourt. Palladio's version of the Tuscan order (the least elaborate of the orders) was chosen for the low-ceilinged rooms: the Library, Cabinet, and secondary bedrooms. The Dining Room, Tea Room, and the North Piazza represent three versions of the Doric, and the Hall and Jefferon's Bed Chamber, two different examples of the Ionic. Palladio's Corinthian order (the most ornate of the orders used at Monticello) was reserved for the Parlor.

LEFT • The entablature in the Dining Room is the same Doric form used on the exterior of the house except that the frieze is embellished with alternating ox sculls and rosettes.

BELOW • Jefferson's drawing of stair balusters for Monticello dates from the 1770s. In the colonies at that time, the usual form of baluster had a set of turnings that separated the column from the vase. Jefferson chose to simplify the form and merge the column and vase.

ABOVE • The frieze ornaments for the Hall, Parlor, and Jefferson's Bed Chamber are copied from Roman temples illustrated in Antoine Desgodetz's *Édifices antiques de Rome*. The engraving shown is from the Temple of Jupiter the Thunderer and is the source for the Parlor. It depicts the symbols of sacrifice.

Dome Room

Jefferson's inspiration for the first dome on a house in America was the ancient Temple of Vesta at Rome. The room is filled with light and the walls brightly painted with a Mars yellow distemper. The floor was originally painted green. Looking about, one sees the quirks that make the room so distinctive. The plan of the room is not a regular octagon; the circular windows facing the house are raised to the cornice and contain mirrored glass to hide the visible portions of the sloping roof. Then there are the enormous base moldings that seem arbitrary and out of context. But from Jefferson's notes one learns that they represent a classical parapet proportioned not to the room but to the overall height of the building.

The crowning feature is the oculus, the circular opening to the sky, four feet in diameter and twenty-and-one-half feet above the floor. To cover it, Jefferson ordered glass fifty-four inches in diameter—about as large as could be blown at that time. The present installation of a single sheet of blown glass dates from 1989.

ABOVE • Jefferson, who once remarked that "Roman taste, genius, and magnificence excite ideas," turned to antiquity for his inspiration in designing the stepped dome at Monticello. His source was an illustration of the ancient Temple of Vesta—the most sacred shrine in Rome where Vestal Virgins tended a fire, symbolic of the hearth at the center of Roman life.

ABOVE • Inside the Dome Room looking toward the hallway and the half-mirrored windows that hide the roof. In one sense, the interior of Monticello is an essay in architectural juxtaposition. Startling effects are achieved by contrasting scale and by the intersection and even collision of moldings, all of which, when judged as independent features, appear to be proportioned rationally.

"One of My Favorite Amusements"

Thomas Jefferson is reported as saying "Architecture is my delight, and putting up, and pulling down, one of my favorite amusements." Influenced by ancient and modern architectural writings, Jefferson gleaned from both his readings and from his observations in Europe, creating in his architectural designs a style that was distinctively American.

Along with Monticello, Jefferson the architect is best known for his plans for the University of Virginia. Dubbed the "father of our national architecture" by architectural historian Fiske Kimball, Jefferson planned the Virginia State Capitol and was influential in the design of the Federal City in Washington, D.C. In addition, he designed several Virginia houses for friends, as well as his retreat, Poplar Forest. On a larger scale, he planned cities and landscapes. On a smaller scale, he turned his attention to the details of a home, designing clocks, coffee urns, and curtains.

RIGHT • The Roman architectural orders were the basis of much of Jefferson's thinking about proportion and architectural detail. This plate from Palladio illustrates what Jefferson studied.

Since his death, Jefferson's contributions to our national architecture have grown in estimation. In 1987, Monticello and the "academical village" of the University of Virginia were named to the UNESCO World Heritage List, a United Nations compilation of international treasures that must be protected at all costs. In 1993, on the occasion of the 250th anniversary of Jefferson's birth, the American Institute of Architects posthumously granted him its Gold Medal for "a lifetime of distinguished achievement and significant contributions to architecture and the human environment."

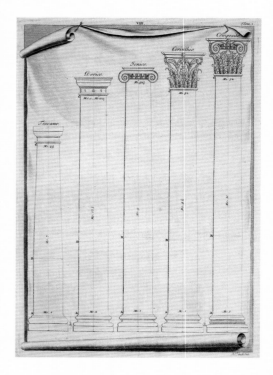

Jefferson advocated using examples of classical Roman architecture for public buildings. His design for the Virginia State Capitol, shown in a watercolor by B. H. Latrobe (ABOVE), was inspired by a first-century Roman temple called the Maison Carrée in Nîmes, France. His 1826 design for the Rotunda, the main building of the University of Virginia (RIGHT), drew inspiration from the Pantheon in Rome (BELOW).

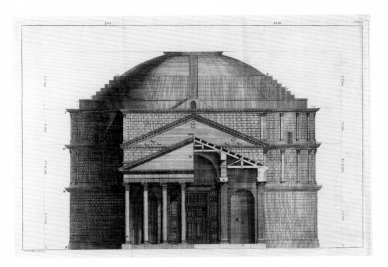

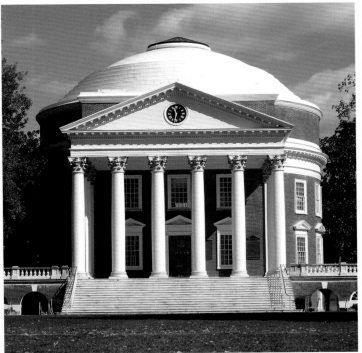

North and South Wings

I nspired by his study of Palladio's villas, Jefferson's early design for Monticello circa 1772 showed domestic functions in two L-shaped wings extending from the main house. It took until 1809 to implement his innovative plan to put the carriage bays, stables, Kitchen, Smokehouse, Dairy, and three slave quarters under the terraces. The terraced wings preserved the mountaintop views, eliminated distracting service buildings from the landscape, and provided sheltered passageways between the house and essential work spaces. Enslaved laborers dug the foundations for the wings.

PAVILIONS

At the end of each wing is a small pavilion with living or office space above, and a work space below. The South Pavilion was the first brick structure built on the mountaintop, while its counterpart, the North Pavilion was constructed over thirty years later.

SOUTH WING

This wing brought together domestic functions relocated from outbuildings on Mulberry Row: the kitchens, Washhouse, Smokehouse, and Dairy. Three rooms in the South Wing became living quarters for the enslaved people working in the house or wings.

KITCHENS

The cellar of the South Pavilion served as Jefferson's kitchen from 1770 until replaced in 1809 by a larger kitchen located at the opposite end of the wing, closer to the house. The old kitchen proved more sophisticated than first believed when Monticello archaeologists unearthed the remains of a stew stove, the eighteenth-century equivalent of a multi-burner cooktop and likely added after Jefferson returned from France. Here Ursula Granger followed by James Hemings and then his brother Peter prepared the renowned Monticello cuisine. It became a washhouse with the

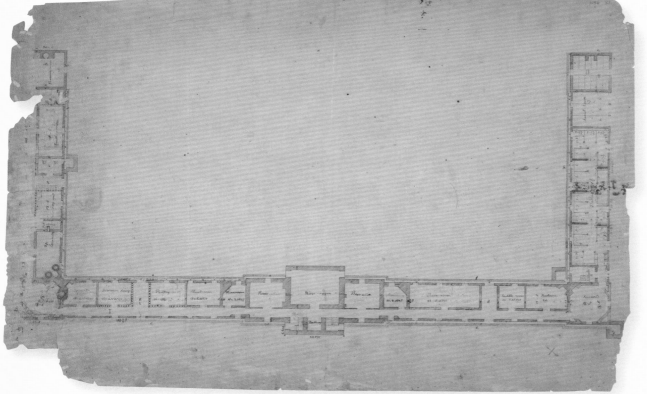

The young Jefferson's circa 1772 plans for the wings were much more elaborate than what was eventually built. He designed temples over the octagonal-shaped spaces at the corners and included many more rooms.

completion of the post-1809 kitchen. The new kitchen had more storage and work space, a large hearth with a bake oven, and an eight-opening stew stove. Enslaved cooks Edith Fossett, Frances Hern, and their assistants continued the tradition of French cuisine at Monticello first introduced by James Hemings.

SMOKEHOUSE AND DAIRY

The Smokehouse moved from Mulberry Row into the South Wing in 1802. Cuts of meat, salted and then hung from the ceiling, were slowly cured by the smoke from the small fireplace. The enslaved kitchen staff carefully supervised this operation as the preserved meats formed the primary source of dietary protein for Jefferson's household and for the enslaved and hired workers. Freshly collected milk cooled in the Dairy, where cream, butter, and cream cheeses were made and stored. These were kept ready for use in the kitchen and on Jefferson's dining table.

LIVING QUARTERS

In addition to workspaces, the South Wing contained three rooms used as living spaces by enslaved workers whose main duties were in the wing or in the main house. The Cook's Room, completed in 1802 and located next to the new kitchen, was occupied by the head cook, first Peter Hemings

and then Edith Fossett and her husband blacksmith Joseph Fossett and their family. Sally Hemings and her children occupied one of the other two 14' × 15' rooms designated for enslaved house servants. Overseer Edmund Bacon described these rooms as "very comfortable, warm in the winter and cool in the summer."

NORTH WING

This wing contained bays for carriages and stalls for horses used by Jefferson and his many visitors. The icehouse was located under the North Terrace and the cellar under the North Pavilion may have served for storage of firewood or supplies prior to its use as a washhouse after 1818.

ICEHOUSE

Under the North Terrace was the coldest spot on Monticello Mountain and thus chosen by Jefferson as the location for his icehouse. He gave instructions for a round structure, sixteen feet in diameter and sixteen feet deep, which was constructed in the winter of 1802–3. Straw and wood chips insulated the ice hauled by wagon loads from the Rivanna River. The ice generally lasted through most of the summer to chill fresh meats, butter, and wine and make ice cream.

Restoration of Monticello

Monticello has forever been a work in progress, beginning with Jefferson's initial direction and extending through the care of the Levy family, from their purchase in 1834 until their sale to the Thomas Jefferson Memorial Foundation in 1923. Since acquiring Monticello, the Foundation has been committed to the preservation and restoration of Jefferson's mountaintop home so that it reflects his architectural vision, including the gardens, work spaces, and Mulberry Row.

The evidence-based scholarly restoration that has marked the stewardship of this World Heritage Site began with the restoration of the North Wing in 1938. Since then, generations of architects, historians, restoration experts, curators, and archaeologists have restored or re-created rooms in the house, the South Wing, the terraces, the Venetian Porches that flanked Jefferson's Greenhouse, and the North and South Pavilions. Landscape restoration included the gardens around the house, the Grove, the orchards, the Vegetable Garden with its stone retaining wall, Mulberry Row, the Garden Pavilion, and Jefferson's "roundabout" road system.

A major undertaking was the roof restoration in 1991–92. The Foundation faithfully restored what was, in its time, one of the most complex roofing systems on any house in America, especially with its iconic dome.

ABOVE • William Roads made this first known photograph of Monticello in 1867–68.

ABOVE • Restoration during the period 1938–55 was directed by Fiske Kimball (RIGHT), chairman of the Foundation's restoration committee, and the architect Milton Grigg (LEFT).

LEFT • The North Terrace was reconstructed in 1941.

RIGHT • The Dome under restoration in 1991. The framing was found to be original, but the steps were reconstructed. Plans for the restoration were guided by Jefferson's notes calling for the Dome to be based on Palladio's delineation of the Temple of Vesta in Rome.

ABOVE • When existing Jefferson-era architectural elements need to be removed for conservation, such as this circa 1800 frieze board, they are carefully repaired and then reinstalled in the same location.

LEFT • Jefferson had two dumbwaiters that delivered wine from the Wine Cellar to the Dining Room. One of the dumbwaiters was reconstructed in 2010 based on surviving fragments.

Restoration of Monticello
Mountaintop Project

In 2013, the Foundation launched the Mountaintop Project, an all-encompassing $35 million, five-year effort to restore Monticello as those who lived there knew it, and to tell the stories of the people—enslaved and free—who lived and worked on the 5,000-acre plantation.

Initiated by a transformational gift from David M. Rubenstein, the landmark project made possible a total of nearly 30 newly restored or re-created spaces and exhibits. Iconic rooms on every level of the house and important buildings on Mulberry Row received updated interpretation or were restored for the first time.

On May 2, 2015, the Foundation unveiled the first phase of the project: the restored and refurnished upper floors of the house, the Kitchen Road, and two log buildings along Mulberry Row.

On June 16, 2018, the culmination of the project was celebrated in conjunction with the twenty-fifth anniversary of the *Getting Word* Oral History Project. The final phase featured the restoration of two original Jefferson buildings on Mulberry Row (the Stable and the Textile Workshop) and of Jefferson's private suite in the house; the reconstruction of the North and South Wings, the South Pavilion, and the original kitchen under the South Pavilion; and the opening of the exhibit "The Life of Sally Hemings" in a restored slave quarters where she likely lived.

ABOVE • Monticello's curators and restoration experts undertook a comprehensive study and renovation of Jefferson's private suite of rooms, with more historically accurate paint colors, furnishings and accessories.

BELOW • The log Storehouse for Iron was the first building to be reconstructed on Mulberry Row as part of the Mountaintop Project. The original building was built in 1792.

BELOW • An original circa 1775 East Portico column was conserved and repainted.

RIGHT · The North Bedroom, believed occupied by Jefferson's grandsons, is just one of a series of furnished rooms on the upper floors that are now open to the public. These newly opened spaces tell the story of private life at Monticello.

BELOW · The 1809 Stable was one of two Jefferson-era buildings on Mulberry Row restored during the Mountaintop Project.

ABOVE · One of the most important accomplishments of the Mountaintop Project was the restoration and reconstruction of the physical presence of slavery on Mulberry Row and in the North and South Wings. Inside a slave quarters in the South Wing, visitors will encounter a multimedia exhibit—"The Life of Sally Hemings"—that relies on the words of Sally Hemings's son Madison to explore her life and legacy.

A Look Inside
MONTICELLO

By SUSAN R. STEIN, *Richard Gilder Senior Curator, Special Projects,*
and EMILIE JOHNSON, *Assistant Curator*

Throughout his long political career in distant New York, Philadelphia, Paris, and Washington, Thomas Jefferson longed "to be liberated from the hated occupations of politics, and to sink into the bosom of my family, my farm, and my books."[1] Even while president, he came back to his beloved Monticello for two months or so during the heat of the summer while the government was in recess. After his retirement from the presidency and a lifetime of political service, Jefferson was at last able to return to Monticello for good. He was joined there by his daughter Martha and her husband Thomas Mann Randolph Jr. and six of their eight children (three more were born later). Jefferson's mountaintop home became a hive of activity where relatives and friends might visit for weeks at a time.

Monticello was sometimes besieged with visitors, many of whom arrived without advance notice. Martha Jefferson Randolph, who managed the plantation household, complained to one of her daughters

that they recently had "20 persons to dinner in the dining room and 11 children & boys in my sitting room 31 persons in all."[2] Poplar Forest, Jefferson's plantation retreat, offered a respite from the duties of hospitality. One of the granddaughters wrote her mother from Poplar Forest that "fortunately we have not been much interrupted by company."[3]

When we consider Monticello today, our thoughts often turn, with good reason, first to Jefferson's remarkable architectural achievement and to his wide-ranging collection of paintings, sculpture, and Native American artifacts he assembled within the house. The house, however, was more than a mere showpiece; it set the scene for daily social and family life during Jefferson's lifetime. Jefferson's writings, family letters, and the accounts of visitors reveal a rich domestic life alive with activity. The sections that follow seek to illuminate that activity, and to suggest how Monticello's rooms were arranged and used during Jefferson's retirement.

Monticello's Hall served as a museum where Jefferson exhibited a wide range of objects that amazed his visitors. One visitor remembered the "strange furniture of its walls" and the "curiosities which Lewis and Clark found in their wild and perilous expedition."

Hall

Visitors to Monticello were enthralled by the Hall and the "strange furniture of its walls"—maps, antlers, sculpture, paintings, Native American artifacts, and minerals.[4]

The atmosphere was markedly different from the houses of other Virginia gentry, whose halls were typically hung with ancestral portraits. Jefferson regarded the double-storied Hall as a museum where he could educate his visitors while they waited to meet him or his family. After being received by Burwell Colbert, the slave houseman and butler, visitors might have rested in the twenty-eight Windsor chairs and taken notice, as did one visitor, of the "odd union" of "a fine painting of the Repentance of Saint Peter" with an Indian map on leather.[5] One visitor, welcomed by Jefferson, likened the Hall's "innumerable relics" to "the adornments of Romeo's apothecary shop where a tortoise hung, an alligator stuffed …"[6] Another noted that Jefferson himself showed guests a draft of the Declaration of Independence, "scored and scratched like a schoolboy's exercise." Visitors were struck not only by the unusual grass green color of the floor, suggested by artist Gilbert Stuart as Jefferson sat for his portrait in 1805, but especially by the double-faced Great Clock, which still shows the second, minute, hour, and day of the week.

ABOVE • The interior face of the Great Clock, designed by Jefferson. Heavy cannonball-like weights power the clock and mark the day of the week as they descend from Sunday to Thursday, and then disappear through holes cut in the Hall floor. The markers for Friday and Saturday are located in the cellar.

Parlor

Visitors entered the Parlor through the single-acting, double glass doors. The "large and lofty salon, or drawing room" described by the Marquis de Chastellux was the principal social space where family members gathered and invited their guests

Family tradition suggests that Jefferson was a keen chess player. He taught the game to his granddaughter Ellen, and they sometimes played outside under the trees in the summertime. Jefferson owned several sets of chess pieces, including this English-style example.

to join them as they made music, read, played games, wrote letters, or took tea. One of the granddaughters, Virginia Randolph Trist, recalled the games that were played there. "When it grew too dark to read, in the half hour which passed before the candles came in, as we all sat round the fire, he [Jefferson] taught us several childish games, and would play them with us."[7] Conversation was an important social activity as well as an exchange of ideas. One visitor noted that "the ladies returned with the tea-tray a time before seven, and spent the evening with the gentlemen; which was always pleasant, for they are obviously accustomed to join in the conversation, however high the topic may be."[8]

The room was furnished for multiple uses and its movable furniture was configured to suit the activity and number of persons present. It was used daily as a sitting and music room and also hosted family weddings and christenings. A large number of different kinds of chairs and a sofa could accommodate family and visitors who assembled there in the late afternoon and early evening. The chairs were sometimes arranged in a circle for the Randolph children for reading and games. Jefferson's favored chair was a Campeche, or siesta, chair in which he often read. Granddaughter Virginia wrote to her sister that a drawing of Monticello would soon reach her and that she "may even fancy that you see Grand-papa's dear figure seated in one of the Campeachy chairs drawn before the door for the sake of the pleasant evening air ..."[9]

Sometimes visitors occupied the family all day long. In 1825, Mrs. Randolph wrote that they were "overwhelmed with company this summer" and that "people going to the Springs have us in the drawing room from 10 to 3, almost everyday."[10] A month later she complained again about the taxing burden of so many visitors, writing "to have a house constantly filled with visitors to be entertained in the day, and accommodate[d] at night, too often 'wears out welcome.' I am very fond of society but *'toujours perdrix'* [too much of a good thing] is insufferable."[11]

OPPOSITE • Surrounded by copies of paintings by Old Masters and portraits of John Locke, Benjamin Franklin, and many others, the family gathered in the Parlor to play games, make music, and read. An Irish visitor noted that this room "during the summer is the one generally preferred by the family, on account of its being more airy and spacious than any other."

Family and guests gathered in
the Dining Room twice a day
for breakfast and dinner. Visitors
noted the books that Jefferson
kept on the mantel to be read
while guests and family gathered.
Granddaughter Ellen Wayles
Coolidge recalled, "In the dining
room where, in winter, we passed
a good deal of time, there was the
low arm chair which he always
occupied by the fire side, with his
little round table still standing
as when it held his book or
his candle."

Dining Room

The Dining Room and adjacent Tea Room were important public rooms where visitors were entertained at breakfast, dinner, and tea. Jefferson's ardent interest in food and wine can be traced to his years in Paris; he recorded recipes—eight of which survive, including one for *biscuits de Savoye.* Monticello's kitchen had a series of French-trained chefs, beginning in 1784 with slave James Hemings, who accompanied Jefferson to France. Hemings was apprenticed to a caterer and then studied pastrymaking in Paris; he trained his brother Peter, who succeeded him. Peter, in turn, helped train enslaved cooks Edith Fossett and Frances Hern, whose cooking was praised by Daniel Webster after he visited in 1824. Webster commented, "Dinner is served half Virginian, half French style, in good taste and abundance."[12]

Monticello's kitchen, located among the wings, or workrooms, on the cellar level, was one of the best equipped in all of Virginia, if not America. In France, Jefferson purchased a large number of utensils, copper pots, and pans. Foodstuffs essential to fine cooking such as "macaroni, Parmesan cheese, figs of Marseilles, Brugnoles, raisins, almonds, mustard, Vinaigre d'Estragon, and other good vinegar, oil, and anchovies" were among the items shipped back from Europe with Jefferson's belongings in 1790. Once Jefferson returned to America, he obtained specialty items from abroad or from grocers in Richmond and Washington. The plentiful Monticello table was also the result of the variety of foods produced and preserved on the plantation. Mutton, pork, beef, and fish were served, and hundreds of varieties of vegetables and fruits were grown, such as cabbage, radishes, carrots, turnips, beets, peas, beans, kale, Jerusalem artichokes, asparagus, apples, berries, figs, peaches, and much more, including oregano, basil, and other herbs. Aside from Jefferson's gardens,

The silver tumbler today known as the Jefferson cup is one of a set of eight that Jefferson had made by silversmith John Letelier in Richmond. The cups were made in part from silver given to Jefferson by his friend and teacher George Wythe. One visitor to Monticello wrote, "The drinking cups were of silver marked G.W. to T.J., the table liquors were beer and cider and after dinner wine."

The Dining Room and Tea Room were equipped with several dumbwaiters. These movable sets of shelves on casters could hold platters of food and clean dishes; they were placed between diners so that they could remove their dirty plates and get clean ones. In the Dining Room, two small elevators, operated by pulleys and also called dumbwaiters, were built into the sides of the fireplace; each could lift a bottle of wine from the wine cellar directly below. "We sat till near sun down at the table, where the dessert was succeeded by agreeable and instructive conversation in which every one seemed to wish and expect Mr. J. to take the chief part," remembered Margaret Bayard Smith of her visit in 1809.

This silver askos, a pouring vessel, was modeled after a Roman bronze askos that Jefferson saw in Nîmes in 1787. Made for Jefferson by Philadelphia silversmiths Simmons and Alexander in 1801, it was dubbed "the silver duck" by family members, who used it as a chocolate pot.

Monticello's larder was supplemented by fish, poultry, eggs, and produce purchased from slaves who often had their own gardens and kept chickens.

Just two meals were served each day, breakfast and dinner. Burwell Colbert, assisted by Israel Gillette, set the table and symmetrically placed platters of food on the table. The breakfast bell rang at about eight o'clock. In 1809, Margaret Bayard Smith reported, "Our breakfast table was as large as our dinner table ... we had tea, coffee, excellent muffins, hot wheat and corn bread, cold ham and butter. ... Here indeed was the mode of living in general [of] that of a Virginia planter."[13] The Randolph children were so well behaved that "you would not know, if you would not see them, that a child was present," Mrs. Smith commented.[14]

A bell was rung to announce dinner, which was served in the late afternoon. The first summoning bell typically rang at three thirty and the second at four o'clock. "The dinner was always choice," George Ticknor wrote, and "served in the French style."[15] Although many family recipes are known, no menus survive for meals at Monticello. However, one guest reported on the menu served at the President's House (now the White House) in 1802: "Rice soup, round of beef, turkey, mutton, ham, loin of veal, cutlets of mutton or veal, fried eggs, fried beef, a pie called macaroni. ... Ice cream very good ... ; a dish somewhat like pudding covered with cream sauce—very fine. Many other jimcracks [nuts and sweetmeats], a great variety of fruit, plenty of wines, and good."[16]

Jefferson's own drinking and eating habits were moderate. His "breakfast is tea and coffee, bread always fresh from the oven, of which he does not seem afraid, with sometimes a light accompaniment of cold meat. Jefferson enjoys his dinner well, taking with his meat a large proportion of vegetables," Webster recalled.[17]

The presentation of dinner noticeably deviated from typical American gentry social practice, which required a servant or slave to serve each diner. Jefferson, eager to minimize the intrusion of slaves, devised a more private and efficient system. A serving door with shelves was installed in the passage adjacent to the Dining Room so that additional serving dishes of food might be placed on it from the passage and later withdrawn from the Dining Room. Jefferson also favored the use of dumbwaiters—sets of shelves on casters—which were placed between and behind the diners so that they could clear their own soiled plates and get clean ones to prepare for the next course. He apparently liked to serve his family and guests himself. Benjamin Henry Latrobe, the architect, observed at the President's House in Washington that "Jefferson said little at dinner besides attending to the filling of plates, which he did with great ease and grace for a philosopher, he became very talkative as soon as the cloth was removed."[18] Guests at the President's House and likely at Monticello, including dignitaries, were seated without regard to rank, or "pell-mell," from the French term *pêle-mêle.*

Beer and cider were served with the meal, but wine was sometimes not poured until the cloth was removed from the table after the main course. Wines from France, Spain, Portugal, Hungary, Germany, and Italy were served, though without the obligatory drinking of "healths," or toasts, as Jefferson believed that the practice encouraged people to drink more than they desired. According to Mrs. Smith, his table was "genteelly and plentifully spread, and his immense and costly variety of French and Italian wines, gave place to a Madeira and a sweet ladies' wine."[19]

To serve food more efficiently as well as to enhance the privacy of the Dining Room, a revolving serving door with shelves was installed between the Dining Room and the north passage. Narrow stairs in the passage lead down to the all-weather passageway, which connects the house to the Kitchen.

Guest Rooms

The two first-floor guest chambers, located along the north passage, were named by the family for the prominent guests who frequently occupied them. The North Octagonal Room was dubbed "Mr. Madison's Room," for two of the most frequent visitors to Monticello, longtime friends James Madison and his wife Dolley. The room features a modern hand-blocked reproduction of the original trellis wallpaper purchased in France. Like many rooms on the first floor, the room also contains a triple-sash window that, when open, forms a doorway to allow easy access to the outside; interior shutters provide insulation and privacy. The bed is built into an alcove, a common feature of the bed chambers.

The Abbé José Correia da Serra (1750–1823), a Portuguese botanist, man of letters, and co-founder of the Academy of Sciences in Lisbon, visited Monticello seven times between 1812 and 1820 while he was Portugal's minister plenipotentiary to the United States. He was such a popular guest that the family called the North Square Room "Correia's Room." Jefferson wrote that he was "the best digest of science in books, men, and things that I have ever met with," and invited him to live at Monticello.

Two frequent visitors stood out for their popularity with Jefferson and his family. The North Octagonal Room (OPPOSITE) was known as Mr. Madison's Room, and the North Square Room as Correia's Room (ABOVE). Rembrandt Peale painted the Abbé's portrait circa 1812.

Jefferson's Sanctum Sanctorum

Close family friend Margaret Bayard Smith employed a popular Latin term, *sanctum sanctorum* (holy of holies), to facetiously describe Jefferson's very private suite of rooms at Monticello. Four connected spaces—the Library, Greenhouse, Cabinet, and Bed Chamber—created a comfortable apartment and formed his private domain that was rarely opened to guests. Another visitor, Sir Augustus John Foster, recognized that "it was here he sat and wrote and he did not like of course to be disturbed by visitors," but lamented that "if the Library had been thrown open to his Guests, the President's Country house would have been as agreeable a Place to stay as any I know."[26] Foster was seeking the equivalent of the English tradition of using a country house library as a sitting room, but Jefferson's arrangement did not allow for guests.

The Library (OPPOSITE) was part of an interconnected suite of Jefferson's private rooms. His copy of *The Federalist* (BELOW) was part of his library at the time of his death in 1826.

LIBRARY

Jefferson wrote to John Adams, "I cannot live without books."[27] He had just sold most of his extensive library—approximately 6,500 volumes—to the national government to begin rebuilding the Library of Congress, which was burned during the War of 1812. Ten wagons carried the books to Washington in the spring of 1815. His library was described as "extensive and contains, as might indeed be expected, a vast collection of rare and valuable works, on all subjects, and in all languages."[28] Visitors, when admitted, were fascinated with the "valuable and curious books—those which contained fine prints etc.— ... a vol[ume] of fine views of ancient villas around Rome ... an old poem written by Pierce Plowman & printed 250 years ago ... More than two hours passed most charmingly away."[29] After the sale to Congress, he assembled another, smaller library.

In addition to stacked open-faced boxes filled with books, "a little closet contains all his garden seeds," Margaret Bayard Smith wrote. "They are in phials, labeled and hung on little hooks. Seeds such as peas, beans, etc., were in tin cannisters—but everything labeled and in the neatest order."[30]

GREENHOUSE

An inspired gardener, Jefferson kept flowers, plants, and flats for sprouting seeds in the Greenhouse. It was "divided from the other by glass compartments and doors; so that the view of the plants it contains, is unobstructed."[31] The Greenhouse also held an aviary, home to Jefferson's pet mockingbirds.

Jefferson also appears to have kept a chest of tools and workbench here. He had the skills to repair his scientific instruments and carry out "any little scheme of the moment in the way of furniture or experiment," a granddaughter recollected. Isaac Jefferson, a slave, remarked that Jefferson was "as neat a hand as you ever saw to make keys and locks and small chains, iron and brass."[32]

CABINET

In his Cabinet, or study, Jefferson was "surrounded by several hundred of his favourite authors ... and every luxury and accommodation a student could require. This

apartment opens into a green-house, and he is seldom without some geranium, or other plant beside him."[33] Satisfying Jefferson's "supreme delight" in the sciences, here were "mathematical instruments, mineralogical specimens, and the like, which indicated the varied intellectual tastes and pursuits of the proprietor."[34]

Correspondence occupied Jefferson for a large portion of every day. In retirement, the hardship of responding to all the letters he received tired him. He admitted to John Adams in 1817, "From sun-rise to one or two o'clock, and often from dinner to dark, I am drudging at the writing table." His letters—copied by a variety of polygraphs, or copying machines—were stored in five filing cabinets made in Monticello's own joinery as well as in additional wooden cartons.

In December 1824, Daniel Webster wrote, "Mr. Jefferson rises early in the morning, as soon as he can see the hands of his clock, which is directly opposite his bed, and examines his thermometer immediately, as he keeps a regular meteorological diary. He employs himself chiefly in writing till breakfast." Shown above is the obelisk clock used by Jefferson in his Bed Chamber that he had made to his specifications by Parisian clock maker Chantrot in 1790.

JEFFERSON'S BED CHAMBER

Daniel Webster reported that Jefferson's practice was to arise at dawn, "as soon as he can see the hands of his clock, which is directly opposite his bed," and then examine the "thermometer immediately, as he keeps a regular meteorological diary."[35] The black marble obelisk clock he designed and had made in Paris by Chantrot still sits on a shelf at the foot of his bed alcove; one of his several thermometers is placed on a nearby wall.

On July 4, 1826, the fiftieth anniversary of the day and time that Congress approved the Declaration of Independence, Jefferson died in his bed at nearly one o'clock in the afternoon. John Adams died later that same day, believing that Jefferson still survived.

With an eye toward "comfort and convenience," Jefferson furnished his Bed Chamber with stylish silk curtains and marble-topped tables. These imported furnishings mixed well with the Virginia-made bureau his wife used during their marriage and furniture made at Monticello.

During his daily inspections of the plantation, Jefferson carried various portable instruments for making observations and measurements, including pocket-size scales, drawing instruments, a thermometer, and a surveying compass. To record these measurements and other notes, Jefferson carried ivory notebooks on which he could write in pencil. At his writing table in his Cabinet, he later copied the information into any of seven books in which he kept records about his garden, farms, finances, and other concerns.

LEFT · Inside Jefferson's pockets (CLOCKWISE FROM UPPER RIGHT): key ring and trunk key, gold toothpick, goose quill toothpick, pocket knife, ivory rule, watch fob, steel pocket scissors, and red-leather pocketbook.

ABOVE · This English pocketknife, likely carried in Jefferson's coat pocket, has twelve tools, including saw, file, drill, corkscrew, and knife blades.

109

Two sets of narrow stairs, just two feet wide, provide the only access to the upper floors. Visitor Anna Thornton recalled, "When we went to bed we had to mount a little ladder of a staircase about 2 feet wide and very steep."

Second and Third Floors

During Thomas Jefferson's retirement, at least thirteen members of his family, enslaved people, and guests occupied the crowded, busy bedrooms and passages on the second and third floors of Monticello. His daughter Martha Jefferson Randolph lived there with at least three of her sons, four of her daughters, a son-in-law, three infants, and Jefferson's youngest sister. Martha's other married children and their spouses and children were frequent guests. Residents of the upper floors belonged to four generations, from infants to the elderly. In the passages and up and down the stairs, enslaved maids removed dirty clothes and bed linens and brought water, fuel for the stoves, and clean textiles for the comfort of the family members. When Monticello was full of guests, Jefferson's family members probably would change sleeping arrangements to accommodate overnight visitors. Newly refurnished in 2015 as a part of the Mountaintop Project, the rooms reveal family dynamics and offer a foil to the tranquility that Jefferson cultivated in his private suite on the first floor.

Architecturally, the rooms and passages of the second and third floors reflect private, domestic functions. With the exception of the Dome Room, the ceilings are lower and the moldings simpler than in the rooms on the first floor. Instead of fireplaces with decorative mantelpieces, iron stoves heated the bedrooms on the second story. The rooms on the third story had no heating elements at all. On cold, winter days, occupants of these rooms probably spent most of their time elsewhere in the house.

The private spaces and their functions inform us about Monticello's residents— whether the women, children, guests, or enslaved servants—and their relationships. On the second floor, bedrooms on the north side of the Hall accommodated a combination of visitors and Jefferson family members. Periodically, enslaved people slept in the North Passage, such as Patsy, who sometimes slept under the window. Martha Jefferson Randolph, her daughters, young sons, and grandchildren occupied bedrooms on the south side of the Hall. Even Martha Jefferson Randolph sometimes had to cede her private space—two of her daughters moved in to her room for a time. The third-floor bedrooms probably housed older grandsons and sometimes Thomas Mann Randolph, estranged from his wife.

Second Floor, North Side

NORTH OCTAGONAL ROOM

Jefferson's youngest sister, Anne Scott Jefferson Marks (1755–1828), came to Monticello as a childless widow in 1812 and may have occupied the North Octagonal Room for some of her sixteen-year stay at Monticello. Aunt Marks seemed like a busybody and a hypochondriac to her younger relations, whose letters reveal frequent exasperation with her. She lived at Monticello until her death, outliving her brother by just over two years. Scilla, an enslaved woman who often provided health care to the women in Jefferson's family, was Anne Marks' primary caregiver in her final illness. Both women were born at Shadwell. Scilla was seven years younger than Anne; they knew each other for almost their whole lives.

Silhouettes of Martha Jefferson Randolph's five daughters and her aunt flank a mirror that hangs above a marble-topped commode similar to the one she used in France.

Second Floor, South Side

SOUTH OCTAGONAL ROOM

Martha Jefferson Randolph used this bedroom, conveniently adjacent to the Nursery and just up the stairs from her father's private suite. In 1822, she had a plan for reorganizing her room, yet at forty-nine years old, the mother of eleven children, one of the best educated women in America, and the manager of a large plantation household, she had to petition her father for permission to move her bed out of the alcove and add a closet. She finally prevailed and wrote to her daughter Virginia,

> *I have at last succeeded in having My alcove turned into a closet and you have no idea how much it has added to My comfort. I laid regular siege to Papa who bore it in dignified silence for some time, but I gave it to him for breakfast, dinner, and supper, and breakfast again till he gave up in despair at last, and when it is painted it will not disfigure the room at all ...*

LEFT • Martha Jefferson Randolph's leather covered box, circa 1800, was made in England and held notes, jewelry, and small locks of hair.

APPENDIX

Until 1825, five of Jefferson's six granddaughters resided full-time at Monticello. They had to share bedrooms. Situated directly above Jefferson's Cabinet, the Appendix is a small room that was occupied by at least two of Jefferson's granddaughters. Ellen

Randolph Coolidge remembered being in this room and hearing her grandfather "frequently thus singing the old Psalm tunes, or the Scotch melodies." The Randolph women were prolific correspondents. Their letters reveal the household in great detail, including the granddaughters' habits of leaving books, notes, clothing, and accessories all over the house. They thought their messiness had a purpose—keeping enslaved maids busy picking up after them. After leaving Monticello, Ellen realized that hired maids in Boston did not work the same way.

NURSERY

In 1796, Jefferson used the word "nursery" in his remodeling notebooks, suggesting that he intended his children and grandchildren to spend considerable time with him in the expanded Monticello. A nursery was commonly understood as any room where a child slept, but having a dedicated space for children was unusual for the period. In the Nursery at Monticello, infants and young children slept, played, and were cared for in this space, tended by Priscilla Hemmings and other enslaved nurses.

ABOVE • Jefferson's granddaughter Septimia used this cabinet as her dollhouse.

OPPOSITE • Likely a hive of activity, the Nursery was where the youngest children slept, ate, and learned such important skills as sewing.

Third Floor

DOUBLE ALCOVE ROOM

Although documents have not confirmed the occupants of the large, unheated bedroom with two bed alcoves, we believe that young men, particularly Jefferson's grandsons, may have stayed here. At Monticello, young men may have primarily

occupied their bedrooms for sleeping, spending the majority of their time elsewhere in the house, at school, or outside, riding horses or roaming the plantation. Unlike young women, whose chores and education, except for gardening, largely took place indoors, young men in Jefferson's household combined a classical education with outdoor exercise.

Dome Room and Cuddy

Based on classical sources, the Dome Room made a powerful architectural statement, with its Mars yellow walls, grass green floor similar to the one in the Hall, and large-scale architectural moldings. Its primary function was to be viewed from the outside, yet this "noble and beautiful apartment," as described by one visitor, served myriad purposes. In 1809, this room was unfurnished, disappointing the admiring visitor who thought "it might be made the most beautiful room in the house." Grandson Thomas Jefferson Randolph lived here with his new wife for a short time after their 1815 wedding. In 1826, and possibly before, it was used for storage.

A small, unfinished attic space adjoined the Dome Room, which in 1823 was claimed by two of Jefferson's granddaughters, Virginia and Cornelia, as their private hideaway. They christened this space their "Cuddy," a term for a small room derived from a cuddy or cabin on a ship. Jefferson's granddaughters were both intellectually and practically educated. They studied classical subjects unavailable to most women of the time, utilizing their grandfather's library to study history, languages, and philosophy. The other side of their education, the practical side, trained them in plantation household management and included taking one-month shifts of running the household, managing enslaved people, ordering menus and supplies, and serving as the primary hostess. They vastly preferred their intellectual studies and bemoaned the duties that took them away from their books. The Cuddy, once outfitted with

OPPOSITE • View from the hallway looking into the Dome Room and the adjoining attic space called the Cuddy by Jefferson's grand-daughters. Of the Dome Room itself, Margaret Bayard Smith wrote, "He afterwards took us to the drawing room, in the dome 26 or 7 feet in diameter. It is a noble and beautiful apartment, perfectly round with 8 circular windows & a skylight. It was not furnished, & being in the attic story is not used, which I thought a great pity."

The Cuddy or attic room facing the West Lawn provided the secluded refuge sought by the studious sisters Cornelia and Virginia Randolph.

old furniture, provided Virginia and Cornelia a space in modest imitation of their grandfather's Cabinet downstairs, where they could hide away to read and write. Virginia provided the most detailed description of the furnishings of any upstairs room:

Cornelia's ingenuity in conjunction with mine formed steps from the dome into this little closet with a pile of boxes, and having furnished this apartment with a sopha to lounge upon, though alas! without cushions, a high and low chair and two small tables, one for my writing desk, the other for my books; and breathing through a broken pane of glass and some wide cracks in the floor; I have taken possession with the dirt daubers, wasps and humble [sic] bees ... [36]

Their pursuit for privacy in a teeming household demonstrates the rarity of quiet spaces to the many occupants of the second and third floors.

North and South Pavilions

Construction of the South Pavilion, believed to be the oldest building at Monticello, began in the late summer of 1770. Jefferson likely occupied it by November 1770 and brought his bride, Martha Wayles Skelton Jefferson, here in January 1772; their first child, Martha, was born in the building later that year. The Jeffersons lived in the South Pavilion—what Jefferson called the "outchamber"—while the main house was under construction.

In 1808, Jefferson stored his law books in the South Pavilion, and in 1809, Charles Bankhead, a grandson-in-law, studied law there. Later, the building was sometimes used for music and dancing. The lower level functioned as Monticello's kitchen until

1808, when it was remodeled as a washhouse, or laundry.

Completed by 1809, the North Pavilion was occupied by Thomas Mann Randolph Jr., Jefferson's son-in-law, and used as a study. Both pavilions are linked to Monticello by L-shaped wooden terraces, under which are located the house's wings, or service rooms, including the Kitchen, Smokehouse, stables, Dairy, storage cellars, icehouse, ware room, and some slave quarters. Above these workspaces, on the terraces, family and guests could walk in the evening, or sit on Windsor chairs or benches made to Jefferson's design. The outdoor porticoes and terraces enhanced the enjoyment of Monticello's landscape and gardens, in effect extending the living space of this busy house.

Martha Wayles Skelton Jefferson

Martha Wayles Skelton Jefferson (1748–82) was a young widow when she and Jefferson married on January 1, 1772. She was born at The Forest, the tidewater Virginia plantation of her father, John Wayles. Her mother, Martha Eppes Wayles, died a week after her birth.

Martha Wayles was married first to Bathurst Skelton in 1766, who died two years later; their three-year-old son died six months before she married Jefferson. No portraits of Martha Jefferson are known. Visitors to Monticello described her as a "mild and amiable wife" and "a very agreeable Sensible and Accomplished Lady." Martha played the harpsichord and pianoforte and managed the enslaved people who carried out domestic activities at Monticello. She recorded her involvement with poultry, butchering, and candlemaking in an account book, one of the few surviving documents in her hand.

She and Jefferson had six children, but only two daughters, Martha and Mary, lived to adulthood. After copying these lines from Laurence Sterne's *Tristam Shandy*, Martha died four months after the birth of her last child:

> *Time wastes too fast: every letter*
> *I trace tells me with what rapidity*
> *life follows my pen. The days and hours*
> *of it are flying over our heads like*
> *clouds of windy day never to return–*
> *more. Every thing presses on–*

Jefferson was insensible for weeks after the loss of his "cherished companion."

LEFT • The South Pavilion, completed in the fall of 1770, was the first brick building at Monticello.

Furnishing
MONTICELLO

Jefferson as Consumer and Collector

BY SUSAN R. STEIN
Richard Gilder Senior Curator, Special Projects

The wide array of furnishings and art at Monticello reflects not only Thomas Jefferson's taste and interests but also his exceptional access to an increasing variety of consumer goods in America and Europe. Inspired first by what he learned in books and later by what he experienced firsthand in France, Jefferson aspired to join an educated international elite. Monticello's furnishings—its decorative arts, paintings, natural history specimens, scientific instruments, and Native American artifacts—very much expressed Jefferson's ambitious vision for his plantation home and the nation.

Jefferson's aspirations for Monticello required both unusual knowledge and energy; he looked beyond Virginia to inspire and to realize his goals to create an educated citizenry equipped to build and sustain the new nation. Monticello's complex neoclassical design, for example, required him to secure the involvement of skilled house joiners from distant places to construct the house. Likewise, Jefferson's cosmopolitan taste roused his interest in fashionable furnishings from Philadelphia, New

York, and especially Paris. Charlottesville, a small town in rural central Virginia, was distant from the marketplaces of Richmond and Williamsburg, and Jefferson's excursions to urban centers became shopping expeditions. Like many planters of his day, Jefferson also ordered a variety of goods from makers as distant as London. Toward the end of his life, he turned to his own joiners, free and enslaved, to make a great deal of furniture for Monticello and Poplar Forest, his tobacco plantation and retreat in Bedford County, Virginia.

Before Jefferson's journey to Europe in 1784 at the age of forty-one, his knowledge of the larger world was confined to America's Eastern Seaboard. He briefly toured Philadelphia in 1766 and lived there intermittently in 1775 and 1776 while a delegate to the Continental Congress. He lived in Williamsburg and frequented its shops. As a representative to the Confederation Congress, he resided in Annapolis in 1783 and 1784.

Jefferson in Paris

When he was appointed to serve as minister plenipotentiary in May 1784, he made arrangements to travel to France with his oldest daughter Martha and James Hemings, an enslaved man. Jefferson sailed on the *Ceres* on July 5, arriving in Paris on August 6, 1784; his frame of reference—and Monticello's appearance—was forever altered by his experience there. The contrast between the great capital and the young cities of America was stunning. Upon arriving in Paris, Jefferson stayed in the Hôtel d'Orleans near the vibrant Palais Royal, an architectural arena that was much the center of the city's activity. The old palace had just been transformed by arcaded galleries containing six restaurants, a waxworks, a chess parlor, a theater and theatrical company, and galleries selling Old Masters, medals, and natural history specimens.

OPPOSITE • Objects owned by Jefferson during the years he was in France, from 1784 to 1789, include a visiting card, a pair of stock clasps, and a fragment of a French silk and embroidered waistcoat.

M^r. Jefferson
Ministre Plénipotentiaire
des États Unis d'Amérique.

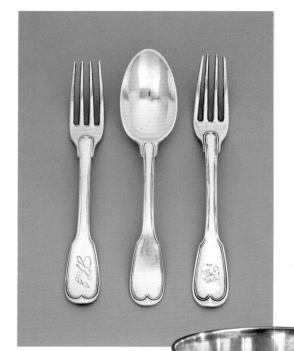

Jefferson noted that the Palais Royal was "one of the principal ornaments to the city and increased the convenience of the inhabitants" while also bringing commercial success to its owners.[1] He clearly took notice of the consumer revolution that made a wide variety of products commonly available to the expanding middle and upper classes. In fact, on his very first day in Paris he bought clothes for his daughter and lace ruffles for himself.[2]

Eager to represent his country in a dignified manner, Jefferson sought accommodations befitting his ministerial rank and suggesting his place in a cultured circle of diplomats and philosophes. He hoped that his government would absorb his expenses, writing that "every other nation has established this" practice, but no reimbursement would ever be made to him.[3]

Jefferson's first real residence was a small *hôtel* (town house) on the cul-de-sac Taitbout in the Chaussée d'Antin. When he realized that he would remain in Paris longer than he had expected, he moved to larger quarters, the Hôtel de Langeac, a fine house designed by the architect Chalgrin at the corner of the Champs-Élysées and the rue de Berri. It served as Jefferson's personal residence and as the American legation. He outfitted his Paris residences as well as he could at his own expense. In Paris he saw and frequented the *marchands merciers*, the shopkeepers who sold everything from fine silks and porcelain to furniture.[4] Most of the extensive purchases he made for his Parisian houses ultimately made their

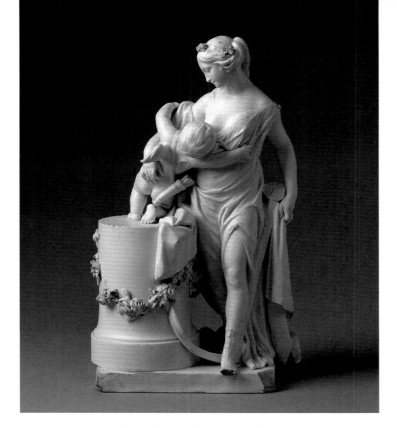

way to Monticello, where they contributed to its sophisticated character. His frequent entries in his personal account books, a detailed packing list of the belongings that followed him back to America in 1790, and many surviving artifacts give a good indication of Jefferson's taste and buying habits. If his tastes seemed extravagant by American standards, they were moderate when compared to the more lavish furniture, porcelain, silver, and silks prevalent in the dwellings of the French elite. Jefferson made his purchases carefully; he bought well but not opulently.

As Jefferson put together his household in a flurry of activity born of necessity, he first assembled the requisite items—linen for sheets and tablecloths, candlesticks, andirons, a coal grate, mattresses, blankets, stoves, carpets, kitchen utensils, lanterns, a coffee mill, silver-plated flatware, lamps and wicks, table wares, matches, and other necessities. On October 16, 1784, the same day that he signed a lease for the house on the cul-de-sac Taitbout, he paid 1,632 livres for "standing furniture."[5] The purchases that he made then would last him a lifetime.

Figurines of classical subjects made of biscuit (unglazed soft porcelain) by Sèvres were popular table decorations for elite households. Of the six or more owned by Jefferson, only two survive, *Hope with Cupid* (ABOVE LEFT) and *Venus with Cupid* (ABOVE RIGHT).

Monticello's Parlor held more than fifty paintings; one visitor described the room as "hung with pictures from floor to ceiling." From Paris, Jefferson wrote James Madison, "You see I am an enthusiast on the subject of the arts. But it is an enthusiasm of which I am not ashamed, as it's object is to improve the taste of my countrymen."

Jefferson, Art Collector

Within three days, Jefferson was buying art for his house. He noted in his account book that on October 19 he purchased "2 small laughing busts, 2 pictures of heads, and 2 pictures half lengths, viz. An Ecce homo & another."[6]

These were among the first acquisitions of what became a consequential collection. In all, Jefferson shipped sixty-three paintings back to America. Jefferson's purpose in collecting art in Paris was mainly didactic, but the choices he made were notably different from the desideratum that he compiled about 1771 for a projected art gallery at Monticello. His early list was primarily made up of classical works of art described in Joseph Spence's *Polymetis*, such as the *Medici Venus*, *Farnese Hercules*, *Apollo Belvedere*, and *Messenger Pulling Out a Thorn*.[7] Jefferson's early interest in sculpture is borne out by two unfinished niches for sculpture at Monticello.

Jefferson's art collecting was undoubtedly influenced by the active artistic scene in Paris. The visual arts filled the biennial Salons, held for about one month beginning on August 25, the king's feast day, in the Salon Carré at the Louvre, where the latest works of the members of the Académie Royale de Peinture et de Sculpture were exhibited. The landscapes, still lifes, genre scenes, portraits, and history paintings were hung frame to frame; history paintings ranked the highest in the well-established hierarchy. Although it is likely that Jefferson attended the Salons of 1785 and 1789, it is only known for certain that he viewed the Salon of 1787, and he was captivated by it. He wrote John Trumbull, the painter, about the Salon's "treasures." "The best thing," he wrote, was "the Death of Socrates by David, and a superb one it is."[8] Jefferson's

Jefferson's collection of paintings included twenty-six presenting biblical themes, including *Salome Bearing the Head of St. John*. Jefferson owned this copy after the original by Guido Reni.

Portraiture was strongly represented in Jefferson's art collection, whether busts, engravings, or paintings. Jefferson called the Enlightenment thinkers Bacon, Newton, and Locke "my trinity of the three greatest men the world had ever produced." Of the three portraits, only Jefferson's 1789 copy of *John Locke*, made after Sir Godfrey Kneller, survives. The Bacon and Newton portraits are contemporary copies of the pictures copied by Jefferson from the Royal Society, London.

intuitive recognition of Jacques-Louis David's talent signaled not only his growing sophistication but also his preference for neoclassicism. David's historical canvases and their ancient subjects appealed powerfully to Jefferson, who later observed, "I do not feel an interest in any pencil but that of David."[9]

Although the price of David's paintings prohibited Jefferson from buying them, he nonetheless put together a sizable art collection, largely of copies. Except for copies of five portraits from the Uffizi Gallery in Florence and five from collections in England, Jefferson acquired most of his collection in just six months between November 1784 and May 1785. He attended at least two sales of paintings, the De Billy sale in November 1784 and the sale of the collection of the late Dupille de Saint-Séverin in the Marais in February 1785. The sources of many purchases are not documented; the entries in his account book indicate that he usually bought more than one picture at a time, perhaps suggesting that his sources were shops or galleries. Of a total of twenty-one purchases, only three of the twenty-one sellers were named—two artists, Jean Valade and Mlle. Adélaïde Labille-Guiard, and Corneillon, from whom Jefferson bought engravings and perhaps paintings.

The paintings cost surprisingly little. Although Jefferson paid as much as 240 livres for an unidentified work by Mlle. Labille-Guiard, a portrait artist whose works were exhibited at the Salons, the average cost per picture was 29 livres, and some cost as little as 6 livres. At the time of purchase, Jefferson rarely noted the subjects, instead only noting "heads" or "half lengths." Most often he simply wrote "pictures," but later he prepared an inventory of the works he owned in which he identified the subject and the artist. Once retired from the presidency, Jefferson took time to annotate the "Catalogue of Paintings &c. at Monticello."

Jefferson's collection of copies favored baroque artists, but Italian Renaissance paintings by Raphael (*Transfiguration and the Holy Family*), Leonardo (*St. John the Baptist*), Pordenone (*Christ before Pilate*), and Titian (*Danäe*) also were represented. Of the few surviving works, three Northern Renaissance paintings are now at Monticello—a copy of Jan Gossaert (*Jesus in the Praetorium*), a copy of Hendrik Goltzius (*St. Jerome in Meditation*), and one of the few original paintings, Frans Floris's *Descent from the Cross*. Baroque artists were better illustrated—Gerard Seghers, Antoine Coypel, Anthony van Dyck, Peter Paul Rubens, Francesco Solimena, José de Ribera, Jean Valentin de Boulogne, Guido Reni, Eustache Le Sueur, and Domenico Zampieri. The one artist that Jefferson clearly favored was Guido Reni; Jefferson owned copies of six of his works—*David with the Head of Goliath*, *Ecce Homo*, *John the Baptist*, *Salome Bearing the Head of St. John* (which Jefferson identified as the work of Vouet), *Head of a Monk*, and *Christ*. The subjects of the paintings fell into three categories: biblical (twenty-six), classical (seven), and biographical (sixteen).

Jefferson acquired a total of twenty-three portraits between 1784 and 1789, including seven terra-cotta patinated plaster busts of Voltaire, Turgot, Franklin, Lafayette, Washington, John Paul Jones, and his own likeness by the eminent sculptor Jean-Antoine Houdon (right). All the portraits in Jefferson's collection depicted men whom Jefferson admired—the Enlightenment figures who provided the underpinnings of his values (Francis Bacon, Isaac Newton, and John Locke), the discoverers and explorers of America (Amerigo Vespucci, Christopher Columbus, Ferdinand Magellan, Hernán Cortés, and Sir Walter Raleigh), and contemporaries (Benjamin Franklin, the Marquis de Lafayette, James Madison, George Washington, Thomas Paine, John Paul Jones, and others).

PREVIOUS PAGES · In addition to its remarkable collection of art, the Parlor features an intricate parquet floor in beech and cherry, one of the first of its kind in America. Philadelphia upholsterer John Rea made the window curtains.

ABOVE · Among the chairs Jefferson purchased in France is a pair of *fauteuils* typical of the Louis XVI period. Jefferson liked to read by the fire while he waited for the family to assemble for the meal. The blue jasperware plaques on the fireplace, made by Wedgwood, were installed during the Levy ownership in the nineteenth century.

French Decorative Arts and Furniture

The art-filled Parisian homes of the well-to-do also contained decorative arts that demonstrated the refined skills of their makers; Jefferson apparently admired what he had seen of the accomplished products of the silversmiths, upholsters, and cabinetmakers. Jefferson's choice of a variety of silver wares, painted porcelain, biscuit figurines (*Hope with Cupid* and *Venus with Cupid* still survive), and candlesticks in the shape of Corinthian columns generally reflected his neoclassical taste. Jefferson himself designed a silver coffee urn and a pair of footed silver goblets; a small silver beaker

ABOVE • The mahogany *fauteuil à la reine* was made by the celebrated French cabinetmaker Georges Jacob. Monticello's collection includes eight of the original suite of chairs. The chairs were originally covered with tapestry featuring neoclassical motifs.

ABOVE • The desk with adjustable top is specifically designed for drawing, with the tabletop adjustable to the angle desired by the user. The sliding supports for the top have had extra notches cut into them to allow the top to be raised higher for Jefferson, who was six feet two and one-half inches tall.

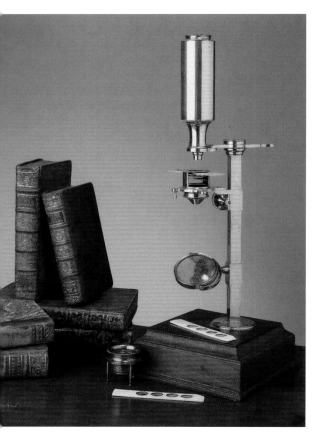

with a gilt-washed interior inspired his later design for a larger version made in Richmond.

Jefferson's preference for simplicity met with further inspiration in the abundant seating furniture placed to accommodate the large-scale entertaining that filled the salons and dining room of the Hôtel de Langeac. Jefferson purchased twenty-two armchairs, twenty-two side chairs, and four bergères, or easy chairs. A good deal of the furniture may have come from three *tapissiers garnisseurs* who supplied household furniture to Jefferson in October 1784. The chairs were of at least five suites, each covered in different upholstery, which included bright pinkish-red, presumably silk damask; blue silk; red Morocco (goatskin); and two shades of *velours d'Utrecht*, a velvet with a pressed design.

The designs of the chairs varied but shared a common neoclassical vocabulary, most with columnar, fluted legs. After 1815, a suite of mahogany *fauteuils à la reine* with saber legs joined the other chairs at Monticello. These streamlined chairs were acquired by Gouverneur Morris from the Parisian *ébéniste* Georges Jacob in 1793 and came to Monticello through his wife, Nancy, a Randolph in-law.

Other furniture at the Hôtel de Langeac included several gaming tables for cards and different kinds of games, such as *jeu de main jaune*. For architectural drawing, Jefferson acquired what his packer Grevin called a *table à pupitre*, a table with a movable top, which eventually was placed in Jefferson's Cabinet and used as a drafting table. It was made by the cabinetmaker Denis-Louis Ancellet, whose workshop was located on the rue Saint-Nicolas, although Jefferson seems to have purchased it from a merchant. He also acquired many smaller tables, some with brass galleries, and marble tabletops.

English Goods

In addition to art and decorative arts acquired in France, Jefferson's belongings included goods purchased during a trip to England during the early spring of 1786. He joined John Adams for a garden tour of country estates and also stayed in London to visit old friends and to finalize a treaty with Portugal. Although Jefferson wrote Lafayette that he was not much disposed to English-made goods, he nonetheless purchased gloves, a hat, a walking stick, knives, maps, cotton stockings, and many scientific instruments. A year later, Jefferson recalled the "splendor of their shops ... is all that is worth seeing in London."[10]

Jefferson, with his keen interest in astronomy, mathematics, and the physical sciences, particularly admired the English mechanical arts, which were "carried to a wonderful perfection."[11] He visited the shops of the finest makers and returned to France with an air pump, compound and solar microscopes, and his first achromatic telescope.[12] These were fine instruments, but not the most costly ornamented models. Jefferson's collection of scientific instruments included a portable orrery, an operating model of the solar system; a theodolite, a surveying instrument, with which he fixed the true meridian of Monticello; a hand magnifier, probably used to examine botanical specimens; a concave mirror for use with his microscopes; a micrometer; a surveying compass; an odometer for measuring distance; various thermometers, including one that he purchased on July 4, 1776, in Philadelphia; and more.

Jefferson ordered two of these London-made "Universal" tables while en route from Paris to Virginia. Also known as a "secret flap table," the table has two sliding leaves that when opened, nearly double the area of the top, suitable for dining, writing, or drawing.

The scales and surveying compass shown here are examples of English-made instruments regularly used by Jefferson. These scales for weighing money and other items he owned were vital to the careful management of his plantations. Jefferson carefully surveyed his landholdings; his interest in surveying was prompted by his father, Peter Jefferson, a surveyor.

Return to America

When Jefferson's application for a leave of absence was granted on August 26, 1789, he waited nearly a month to depart for America. He fully expected to return to Paris, and he placed his secretary William Short in charge of his house and business while he was away. Jefferson sailed with two daughters and slaves James and Sally Hemings on the *Clermont* bound for Norfolk. Even aboard ship, Jefferson managed to make some purchases. He admired a London-made "Universal" table with two sliding leaves that could nearly double the table's total surface area, and asked the ship's captain to obtain two such tables in the "handsomest to be had" French spotted mahogany.[13] Just as Jefferson landed at Norfolk on November 23, a fire broke out on the ship. Remarkably unharmed were the many parcels destined for Monticello containing dozens of bottles of French wines (Frontignans, Rochegudes, Sauternes, and Meursaults), vinegar, olive oil, raisins, books, a bust of Lafayette and a pedestal for it, mattresses, two bedsteads, a guitar, pictures, a clock, clothing, a phaeton, a harpsichord made by Jacob Kirkman, kitchen equipment, and more. The fire was not the only surprise. In Norfolk, Jefferson learned that President Washington had nominated him to serve as secretary of state. Jefferson's time in Europe came to an abrupt end; before long he headed to New York to join the government in its temporary capital.

In New York, Jefferson rented a small house at 57 Maiden Lane. Apparently without hope that his French belongings would arrive quickly, Jefferson equipped his house with looking glasses, flatware, candlesticks from William Grigg; thirty green chairs, presumably Windsors, which would suffice until his French chairs arrived;

Jefferson's travel trunk might have contained his riding boots and socks as well as books, including petit-format books, called octavos and duodecimos. He preferred the smaller books because they were cheaper, compact for traveling, and more easily handled with his wrist, dislocated in 1786.

bedsteads, china and glassware from William Williams; and more. After Jefferson had lived in New York for barely three months, the government recessed and announced its move to Philadelphia, but not before Jefferson bought more chairs, a secretary, and a table from furniture maker Thomas Burling.

Philadelphia

The house that Jefferson leased in Philadelphia at 274 Market Street was just a few blocks away from the American Philosophical Society, the State House, and his own offices at Eighth and Market Streets. When at last his possessions arrived from France, Jefferson paid a "monstrous bill of freight" for the shipment and storage of eighty-six crates; seventy-eight of them remained in Philadelphia while the others were shipped directly to Monticello.[14]

Unpacking was frightfully slow, but after weeks of effort the furniture was installed and the paintings hung. Despite the vast inventory of furniture, Jefferson was still not satisfied; he bought a bedstead from furniture maker John Aitken in January 1791. But Jefferson was not to remain on Market Street, for little more than two years later he decided to move to a country house near Grays Ferry on the Schuylkill River. His "superfluous" furniture was sent to Monticello via Richmond in the spring of 1793. On December 31, 1793, Jefferson resigned his post as secretary of state and returned to Monticello, "liberated from the hated occupation of politics."[15]

Jefferson's full-time attention to his farms, family, and the expansion of Monticello was not long-lived. Public life intervened, and he found himself in Philadelphia again, this time as vice president. His presence there was intermittent, and during his first stay in March 1797 he found time to buy new gloves, a shaving brush, spectacles, and an oiled silk coat, and to make tentative arrangements to

This sewing table was made in the Monticello Joiner's Shop. Reserved for the ladies of the house, it facilitated the never-ending task of sewing and mending.

The Lewis and Clark expedition was central to the formation of Jefferson's collection of Native American objects in what he termed his "Indian Hall." Since most of Jefferson's collection is unlocated today, Monticello commissioned Native American artists to create new pieces based on documentary evidence and surviving period objects. Exhibited works include a medicine bag made from an otter, clothing, and weapons.

ABOVE • Jefferson encouraged the American artist John Trumbull to paint important scenes of American history, including the *Declaration of Independence*. Trumbull began his great work in Jefferson's house in Paris in 1786 but did not complete it until 1818. The engraving exhibited by Jefferson was made by Asher B. Durand in 1820.

RIGHT • The fossilized jawbone of an American mastodon, excavated by William Clark in 1806 in a dig at Big Bone Lick, Kentucky, was also exhibited in the Hall. Jefferson wrote about this rich ancient salt lick on the Ohio River in his *Notes on the State of Virginia*.

RIGHT • A profusion of sculpture, maps, natural history specimens, Old Master paintings, and Native American objects packed the walls of the Hall. In 1818, visitor Salma Hale wrote, "Mr. Jefferson I found on the top of his mountain surrounded with curiosities, and himself not the least. ... His house is filled with paintings and Indian relics, and a view of his rooms affords as much gratification as of a museum."

purchase a bust of himself by the sculptor Giuseppe Ceracchi that he ultimately displayed in Monticello's Hall. Also in the Hall is the Great Clock made by Philadelphia clockmaker Peter Spruck in 1792–93. Over the course of the next three years, Jefferson would patronize the Philadelphia cabinetmaker Joseph Barry, who supplied standing furniture, as yet unidentified. In 1801, President Jefferson engaged the Philadelphia silversmiths Anthony Simmons and Samuel Alexander to craft a silver askos from a wooden model of a Roman pouring vessel that he had admired in 1787 in Nîmes.

Monticello as Museum

The enlargement of Monticello was largely completed by 1809, when Jefferson retired from the presidency. His belongings, a conglomeration of furniture, decorative arts, and various objects associated with his many activities and interests, were assembled in the finished house with an eye toward comfort and convenience. Monticello's interior became a highly idiosyncratic embodiment of his achievements, immense curiosity, and learning, as well as his life as a consumer.

ABOVE • The seven-day clock is powered by cannonball-like weights. Connected to a Chinese gong on the roof, the hours are heard on the mountaintop.

Jefferson collected the best and most accurate maps throughout his lifetime, accumulating more than 350 different maps, navigational charts, and city plans. Eight

Like the Parlor, the walls of the Dining Room were packed with prints and paintings, and also several architectural drawings. Although a copy of Raphael's *Transfiguration* hung there, most of the pictures were American subjects such as Harpers Ferry, Mount Vernon, the port of New Orleans, and Niagara Falls.

or more large engraved wall maps and two Indian maps on leather shared wall space in the Hall with copies of Guido Reni's *David with the Head of Goliath*, Goltzius's *St. Jerome in Meditation*, and other paintings. To portray the natural history of North America, in which he had a keen interest, Jefferson exhibited specimens of many species, notably the antlers of the deer, moose, and elk, the stuffed head of an American argali (bighorn) sheep, and bones of the extinct mastodon.

Jefferson's longtime study of Native Americans was realized in "an Indian Hall I am forming at Monticello."[16] In the Hall he displayed many artifacts of Native American culture and natural history specimens acquired by Lewis and Clark on their expedition, initiated by Jefferson in 1803, as well as other items he collected, including several earthenware figures, a pair of seated stone figures, and a kneeling woman, also carved in stone. The juxtaposition of Western civilization and indigenous American cultures was readily noticed by visitors; in 1815, George Ticknor commented that "in odd union with a fine painting of the Repentance of Saint Peter, is an Indian map on leather."[17]

Sculpture, paintings, engravings, and drawings were principally displayed in the public rooms—the Hall, Parlor, Dining Room, and Tea Room. In addition to the natural history specimens,

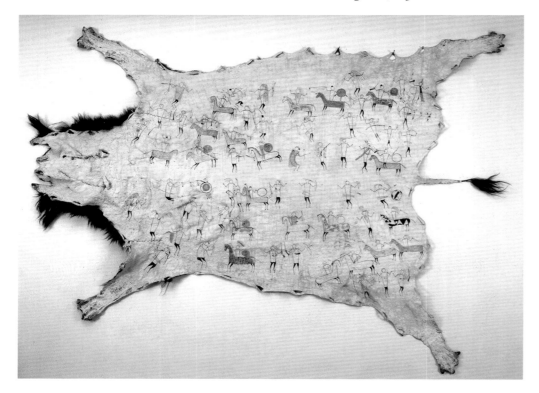

Lewis and Clark sent a buffalo robe to Jefferson in April 1805 from Fort Mandan. George Ticknor saw it in 1815 and described it as "an Indian representation of a bloody battle, handed down in their traditions." This recent interpretation represents the lost original.

Native American artifacts, and maps, the Hall also exhibited eleven paintings. The Parlor contained no fewer than fifty-seven works of art and offered Jefferson another opportunity to instruct his visitors and family.

Among the pieces were thirty-five portraits of the men who had shaped Jefferson's intellectual development as well as American and world history. Their sitters ranged from the "trinity of the three greatest men the world has ever produced"—Francis Bacon, Isaac Newton, and John Locke—to Benjamin Franklin, George Washington, James Madison, John Adams, and David Rittenhouse, the brilliant Philadelphia scientist.[18]

The walls of the Dining Room and Tea Room were similarly crowded with pictures and portraits. The Dining Room held at least ten prints, eleven oil paintings, a watercolor, and three architectural drawings, hung in two tiers, and a plaster of a small sleeping Venus. The top tier exhibited two pictures of the Cynic philosopher Diogenes (d. ca. 320 BC)—*Diogenes in the Market of Athens*, copied after the painting by Peter Paul Rubens, and *Diogenes Visited by Alexander*, by an unidentified artist—as well as nine other paintings that Jefferson acquired in France. Of these, only Jefferson's copy of *The Holy Family* survives today.

The lower tier of the Dining Room pictures primarily focused on American subjects. Among them were a painting by William Roberts, *Natural Bridge*, which Jefferson called "the most sublime of nature's works" in *Notes on the State of Virginia*; engravings of the *Junction of the Potomac and Shenandoah*, *Virginia, Coalbrookdale*

THE NATURAL BRIDGE.

In 1774, Jefferson purchased Natural Bridge, located in Rockbridge County, Virginia, and enthused that it was "so beautiful an arch ... springing as it were, up to heaven, the rapture of the Spectacle is really indescribable!" This 1808 engraving after the painting by William Roberts hangs in the Dining Room.

Bridge, *A View of New Orleans*, and two views of Niagara Falls engraved after John Vanderlyn's paintings.[19]

The Tea Room, which Jefferson referred to as his "most honourable suite," was packed with portraits of patriots, friends, four Roman emperors, and family members. Four terra-cotta patinated busts of John Paul Jones, Franklin, Washington, and Lafayette, all by Jean-Antoine Houdon, dominated the space. A bust of Andrew Jackson by William Rush, a gift, was added to the room in 1820. Sixteen miniature portraits included likenesses of Generals Gates, Dearborn, and Clinton; Meriwether Lewis; John Wayles Eppes, Jefferson's son-in-law; Albert Gallatin; William Burwell, Jefferson's secretary; political allies Caesar Rodney, Gideon Granger, and Joseph Nicholson; and others.

Jefferson's private Cabinet and Library contained all the accoutrements associated with his scientific pursuits, and reading and writing—among them were telescopes, a tall case astronomical clock, the

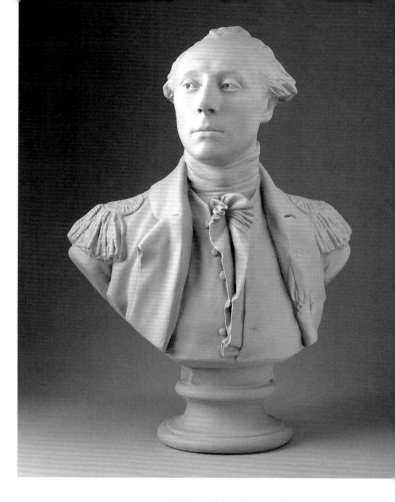

drawing table with a movable top brought from France, a writing table made in Monticello's joinery, a revolving chair, a revolving book stand, pens, drafting instruments, and a polygraph (a copying machine with which Jefferson made duplicates of his outgoing letters). After 1820, Jefferson set up a gallery of plaster busts of the first five presidents.

Furniture Made in the Joiner's Shop

In addition to furniture made in European and American cities, Jefferson used furniture made on his own plantation in the "joiner's shop." These gifted artisans first fashioned architectural elements—doors, windows, balustrades, cornices, and mantels—and turned to furniture after largely finishing the construction of the house in 1809. John Hemmings then took charge when the hired Irish joiners who trained him left. Hemmings, his co-worker Lewis, and other assistants used more than 125 individual planes, chisels, gouges, drawing knives, saws, a brace and bits for drilling holes, rasps, and files in their craft.

Although no labels or marks identify specific pieces of furniture, careful study has revealed about 20 works that can be attributed to the Joiner's Shop. Distinguished by distinctive designs and construction features, these works include filing presses, tables, dumbwaiters, cupboards, a press, chairs, and a seat for Jefferson's phaeton. The designs of these works reflect a variety of sources—principally Jefferson's own furniture from France, Virginia, Philadelphia, and New York—manipulated by Jefferson and his craftsmen in their own way. The resulting style, unusual for its French rather than English influence, has been called "Franco-Piedmont" by furniture historians.

ABOVE · John Hemmings made this clothespress for Anne Scott Jefferson Marks, Jefferson's sister who lived upstairs at Monticello.

LEFT · Family tradition suggests that Jefferson had a role in making this narrow filing press and bookcase that he used in his Bed Chamber.

RIGHT · A cherry, walnut, and southern yellow pine table with a revolving top, attributed to John Hemmings, contains a hidden compartment beneath the top.

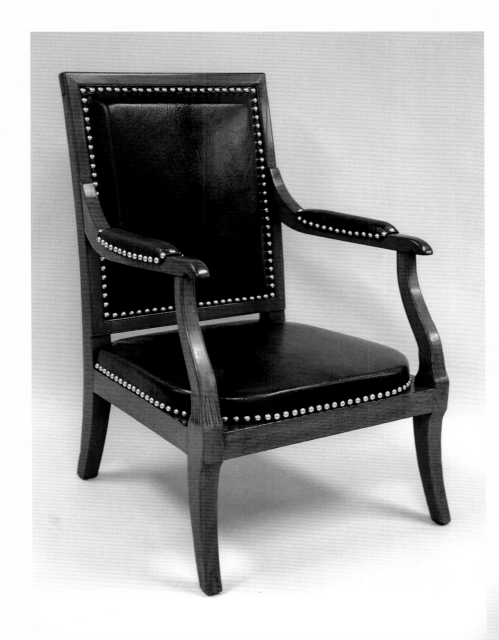

BELOW • Dumbwaiters, some made at Monticello and others from Philadelphia, were used in the Dining Room and Tea Room to ease meal service by limiting the intrusion of servants.

ABOVE • Attributed to John Hemmings, this armchair is an adaptation of the French armchairs in the Parlor made by Georges Jacob.

153

Reading and Writing

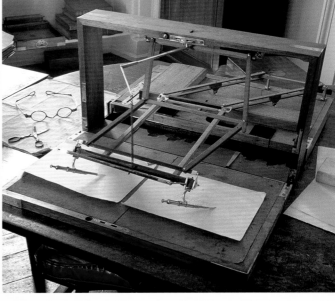

The heart of Jefferson's Cabinet was his novel and highly functional reading and writing arrangement. Jefferson wrote about 19,000 letters; he wrote John Adams that he suffered "under the persecution of leters," calculating that he received 1,267 letters in 1820. Surrounded by filing presses and cartons filled with letters, notebooks, and books, he sat in a revolving chair, rested his legs on a Windsor couch with a tufted cushion, and answered letters using a polygraph on a writing table with a revolving top made in Monticello's joiner shop.

Using a device that he called "the finest inventions of the present age," Jefferson made copies of his letters with a polygraph. As he moved one pen, a second pen produced a duplicate letter on a second sheet. Jefferson acquired his first polygraph in March 1804, and five years later wrote, "I could not live without the polygraph."

This machine and an earlier copying press by James Watt enabled the survival of much of his vast correspondence.

An avid reader and correspondent, Jefferson apparently designed a cube-shaped walnut stand with five adjustable rests that could be deployed for small books, pamphlets, and papers. Jefferson likely used it near his reading and writing arrangement. It may have been made in Monticello's Joiner's Shop.

RIGHT • The revolving stand allowed Jefferson to consult multiple works at once. The revolving top is original; it is now supported by a tripod base matching original evidence.

RIGHT • As he aged, Jefferson's wrist, which he broke while in France, troubled him considerably; he wrote John Adams that "crippled wrists and fingers make writing slow and laborious," even with the use of lead dumbbells and a wrist cushion, designed to strengthen and support his wrists.

Music at Monticello

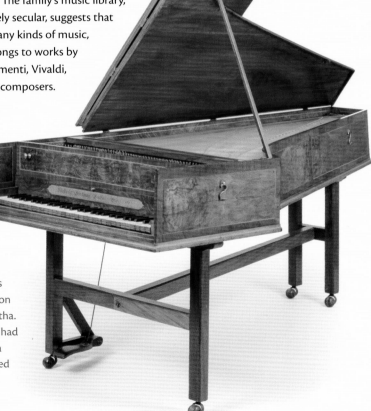

Thomas Jefferson declared that music "is the favorite passion of my soul," and music figured prominently in the daily lives of Jefferson and his family. Until he broke his wrist, Jefferson played the violin—and less frequently, the cello—throughout his life. He claimed that as a youth, he practiced three hours a day, and he played well enough to participate in weekly concerts at the Governor's Palace while a student in Williamsburg. Jefferson purchased several violins, including a portable one he took on his travels. Jefferson shared a love of music with his wife, Martha Wayles Skelton, for whom he purchased a pianoforte during their engagement, and he urged his young daughter Martha to practice music each day, writing, "Do not neglect your music. It will be a companion that will sweeten many hours of life." She played a superb harpsichord with a double set of keys made by Jacob Kirkman in 1786. By 1825 it was in poor condition, and one granddaughter wrote that "it was an old instrument too far gone even to learn on."

The family often gathered in the Parlor for "delightful recreation" after dinner. The family's music library, which was almost entirely secular, suggests that they enjoyed playing many kinds of music, from Scotch and Irish songs to works by Boccherini, Mozart, Clementi, Vivaldi, Corelli, and many more composers.

ABOVE • This cittern, or English guitar, belonged to Jefferson's granddaughter Virginia Randolph Trist.

LEFT • Music for the piano published in Paris and used by the family at Monticello.

RIGHT • This harpsichord made by Jacob Kirkman is similar to one that Jefferson gave to his daughter Martha. However, her instrument had a double set of keys and a "Celestina stop" that added a bowed-string sound.

FEUILLES DE TERPSICHORE
OU
JOURNAL
Composé d'Ouvertures, d'Airs arrangés et d'Airs avec Accompagnement
POUR LE CLAVECIN
Il paroit une Feuille de ce Journal tous les Lundis
Prix 1ll 4f

The Sciences
"My Supreme Delight"

Claiming that "Nature intended me for the tranquil pursuits of science, by rendering them my supreme delight," Jefferson read widely in the sciences, and corresponded frequently with enthusiasts worldwide. His Cabinet was filled with devices for observing, measuring, and recording nature. Influenced by Enlightenment thinkers like Sir Isaac Newton, Jefferson believed that a rational system of order governed the natural world, and that by applying these rules of science, the condition of man could be improved.

Fascinated with almost every aspect of science, Jefferson was particularly interested in those fields like astronomy, which were informed "by the aid of mathematical calculation," perhaps because he noted that "No two men can differ on a principle of trigonometry." As secretary of state, Jefferson established America's decimal system of currency, and argued unsuccessfully for the adoption of a decimal system of weights and measures. President of the American Philosophical Society for seventeen years and the only American of his time to be elected as a foreign associate of the Institute of France, Jefferson was known internationally as a man of learning. Today he is recognized, in the late Jefferson scholar Dumas Malone's words, "as an American pioneer in numerous branches of sciences, notably paleontology, ethnology, geography and botany."

ABOVE • Jefferson's orrery and tellurium, made by London maker William Jones.

ABOVE • Jefferson claimed that his design for a spherical sundial was a "novelty" to him and that it "captivates every body foreign as well as home-bred, as a handsome object & accurate measurer of time." Installed in 2001, this re-creation on the North Terrace is based on his notes and drawings.

ABOVE • A solar microscope projected an enlarged image of a tiny specimen such as the wing of a fly onto a wall or screen.

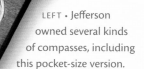

LEFT • Jefferson owned several kinds of compasses, including this pocket-size version.

ABOVE • Jefferson owned a sizeable collection of scientific apparatus. This large and complex air pump from England was of particular note.

ABOVE • Jefferson used this pedestal achromatic telescope for astronomical observations.

RIGHT • For surveying, fixing the true meridian of Monticello, and calculating the position of the features of the Monticello landscape, Jefferson used perhaps the most sophisticated instrument then available, a telescopic theodolite made by Jesse Ramsden.

Gardens
OF MONTICELLO

BY PETER J. HATCH
Director Emeritus of Gardens and Grounds at Monticello

And our own dear Monticello, where has nature spread so rich a mantle under the eye? mountains, forests, rocks, rivers. With what majesty do we there ride above the storms! How sublime to look down into the workhouse of nature, to see her clouds, hail, snow, rain, thunder, all fabricated at our feet! And the glorious Sun, when rising as if out of a distant water, just gilding the tops of the mountains, and giving life to all nature!

—JEFFERSON TO MARIA COSWAY, 1786

Thomas Jefferson's interest in gardening arose from a wide-eyed curiosity about the natural world. He chose the site for Monticello because of its sweeping prospects of the Piedmont Virginia countryside and its intimacy with the busy "workhouse of nature." The landscape was his "workhouse," and the gardens at Monticello became an experimental laboratory. Jefferson approached natural history as a scientist, as an experimenter who aspired to observe and define seemingly all the natural phenomena "fabricated at our feet"—whether the wind direction, the blooming dates of wildflowers, or the life cycle of a destructive insect.

But it was through gardening that he could participate in the motions of this physical world—grafting peach wood or sowing cabbages with his granddaughters. Through horticulture his experiments bore fruit, his landscape assumed shape and form and color, and the drama of the natural world began to unfold under his personal direction.

Garden Scientist

Jefferson's methodical record-keeping reflects his view of the natural world as a biological laboratory. He has been described as the "father of weather observers" for his Weather Memorandum Book, a detailed account of the daily temperatures, rainfall, and wind direction. One of his most enduring legacies was his garden diary, published

Monticello's flower borders come alive in late May with the blooming of sweet William (mixed pink, red, and white) and larkspur (blue).

as *Thomas Jefferson's Garden Book* in 1944.[1] This edition includes not only his personal Garden Book—a "Kalendar" of plantings in his garden, short treatises on soil preparation for grape vines, and meticulous notes on how many "grey snaps" would fill a pint jar—but also extracts from the letters he wrote and received concerning gardening, natural history, and landscape design. Botany, agriculture, even surveying were essential to Jefferson's interest in horticulture and landscape design. An experienced draftsman and capable surveyor, Jefferson repeatedly measured his "Roundabout" roads and composed sketches of his estate. The woodland wildflower twinleaf, or *Jeffersonia diphylla*, was named in Jefferson's honor by the prominent Philadelphia botanist Benjamin Barton in 1792 at a meeting of the American Philosophical Society. Barton proclaimed that Jefferson's "knowledge of natural history ... especially in botany and in zoology ... is equalled by that of few persons in the United States."[2]

When Jefferson wrote "The greatest service which can be rendered any country

is to add a useful plant to its culture," he was expressing his hopes that the introduction of new economic plants could be a means of transforming American society.[3] The staggering number of both useful and ornamental plants grown at Monticello, including over 330 vegetable and 170 fruit varieties,

ABOVE • The globe artichoke (*Cynara scolymus*) was included on one of Jefferson's first lists of vegetables grown at Monticello in 1770. This native of southern Europe is not reliably hardy in Virginia, as Jefferson acknowledged in a letter to his Parisian friend Madame de Tessé in 1805: "we can have neither figs nor artichokes without protection from the winter."

LEFT • Twinleaf (*Jeffersonia diphylla*) is a fitting tribute to Thomas Jefferson's interest in and promotion of natural history. Native to fertile woodlands along the Appalachian Mountains, twinleaf receives its common name from the bisected, or winged, shape of the leaves. Appropriately, the delicate white flowers appear around Jefferson's birthday on April 13.

attests to Jefferson's experimental approach. Monticello was a botanic garden of new and unusual introductions from around the world, and the geographic homes of the plants grown at Monticello reflect the reach of his gardening interests: new species discovered by the Lewis and Clark expedition like the snowberry bush and flowering currant, Italian peach and grape cultivars probably first grown in the New World by Jefferson himself, and giant cucumbers from Ohio twenty-four inches long. Thomas Jefferson envisioned plants as a vehicle for social change.

Jefferson also championed the use of native plants at a time when there were numerous European detractors of the American natural world. Georges Louis Leclerc de Buffon, in his *Histoire naturelle*, argued that the New World's natural

Jefferson organized the "winding walk" border into ten-foot-long sections, each planted with a different species or variety of herbaceous ornamental. Lavender, sweet peas, larkspur, sweet William, *Nicotiana*, and corn poppies take the stage in late spring.

productions—its plants, animals, even native people—were inferior copies of Europe's. The only book Jefferson published during his lifetime, *Notes on the State of Virginia*, was partly an effort to refute Buffon's thesis that the excessive humidity in the United States crippled the biological environment.[4] When serving as minister to France between 1785 and 1789, Jefferson grew Indian corn in his Parisian

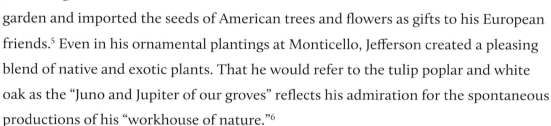

garden and imported the seeds of American trees and flowers as gifts to his European friends.[5] Even in his ornamental plantings at Monticello, Jefferson created a pleasing blend of native and exotic plants. That he would refer to the tulip poplar and white oak as the "Juno and Jupiter of our groves" reflects his admiration for the spontaneous productions of his "workhouse of nature."[6]

American horticulture was in its infancy during Jefferson's lifetime, 1743–1826, and his association with the pioneer gardeners of the United States—nurserymen, writers, plant explorers, botanists, landscape designers, progressive agriculturists, experimental viticulturists—suggests Jefferson's vital participation in the definition of New World plants, gardens, and landscapes. Among his frequent correspondents was Bernard McMahon, curator of the Lewis and Clark expedition, nurseryman, and author of the best gardening book published in America in the first half of the nineteenth century, *The American Gardener's Calendar*, which has been described as Jefferson's horticultural "bible."[7] Furthermore, Jefferson's sponsorship of the Lewis and Clark expedition (which was, in part, considered a botanical exploration) and his role in co-founding both the Albemarle Agricultural Society and American Philosophical

ABOVE • Scarlet runner beans were sowed annually in the Vegetable Garden from 1809 to 1824 and were treasured for their beauty and flavor.

FOLLOWING PAGES • The terraced kitchen garden was Jefferson's major horticultural achievement at Monticello. The one-thousand-foot-long garden was supported by a massive stone wall and overlooked the six-acre fruit garden that included a propagation nursery and the southwest vineyard. These gardens served Jefferson not only as a food source but also as an experimental laboratory. Both the vegetable and fruit gardens were re-created in the early 1980s based on archaeological research and Jefferson's extensive records.

The Garden Pavilion, perched precariously atop the garden wall, reputedly toppled over during a storm soon after Jefferson's death in 1826. A favorite haven for Jefferson to read in the cool of the evening, the pavilion was restored in 1984.

Society set a lofty standard for the promotion of scientific exploration by an American public servant.

"Humanized Horticulture"

For Jefferson, plants were intimately associated with people—friends, neighbors, political allies—and the exchange of seeds, bulbs, and fruit scions represented a token of enduring friendship. This union of gardening and sociability is evident throughout the letters in the Garden Book. Jefferson would chide his daughters and granddaughters for their inattention to the flower beds around the house, while they in turn would report on the latest horticultural dramas taking place at Monticello. Jefferson also engaged in friendly competitions with his neighbors to determine who could harvest the first English pea in spring. The winner then hosted a community dinner, sharing the winning dish (or teaspoon) of peas.[8]

Ellen Randolph Coolidge, one of Jefferson's granddaughters, recalled the heyday of flower gardening at Monticello: "When the flowers were in bloom, and we were in ecstasies over the rich purple and crimson, or pure white, or delicate lilac, or pale yellow of the blossoms, how he would sympathize in

our admiration, or discuss ... new groupings and combinations and contrasts. Oh, these were happy moments for us and for him."[9] The gardens of Monticello hardly existed in a horticultural vacuum, but were nourished generously by a society of local, Virginian, American, and international gardeners.

Jefferson's essential philosophy of gardening was perhaps best summarized in a letter to his daughter Martha after she complained of insect-riddled plants in the Monticello Vegetable Garden: "We will try this winter to cover our garden with a heavy coating of manure. When earth is rich it bids defiance to droughts, yields in abundance, and of the best quality. I suspect that the insects which have harassed you have been encouraged by the feebleness of your plants; and that has been produced by the lean state of the soil."[10] Such commitment to the regenerative powers of soil improvement suggests Jefferson's belief in the wholesome balance of nature and gardening. His response to the damage inflicted by the Hessian fly on his wheat crop revealed more a naturalist's curiosity about an insect's life cycle than a farmer's quest for a successful harvest.[11] When Jefferson wrote that, for a gardener, "the failure of one thing is repaired by the success of another," he was expressing further this holistic approach to horticulture.[12]

In 1807, Jefferson wrote Timothy Matlack, a Pennsylvania fruit grower, and asked for pears, peaches, and grapes. He added, "I shall be able to carry & plant them myself at Monticello where I shall then begin to occupy myself according to my own natural

Herbs, such as the lavender (*Lavandula angustifolia*) flowering above in early June, were included in Jefferson's 1794 memorandum "Objects for the Garden." The list included a variety of culinary and medicinal species that were likely distributed casually throughout the Vegetable Garden, rather than in a formally designed, discrete herb garden.

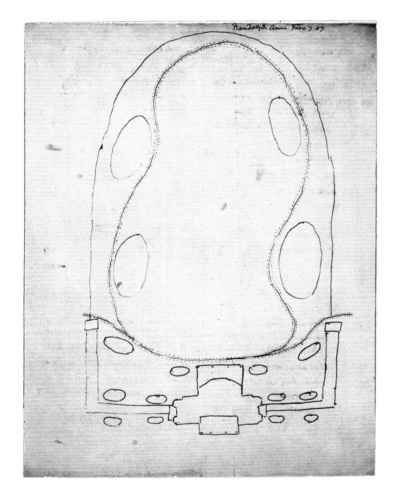

Randolph Anne June 7.07

Jefferson's plan for the winding flower walk in a letter to Anne Randolph, June 7, 1807.

inclinations, which have been so long kept down by the history of our times."[13] The spring of 1807 was perhaps the most painful period of Jefferson's presidency as he suffered periodic migraine headaches that accompanied his involvement in the contentious Aaron Burr treason trial.[14] Even so, it was also the most ambitious and creative gardening period in Jefferson's horticultural career: the vineyards were revived with intensive plantings of twenty-four varieties of European grapes, and the oval flower beds were designed and planted. Gardening was a welcome retreat from the slings and arrows of political life.

Thomas Jefferson was a planter; 1,031 fruit trees were set out in the South Orchard alone. He documented the planting at Monticello of approximately 113 species of ornamental trees and sixty-five shrubs, over 100 species of herbaceous plants in his flower gardens, and 450 varieties of 95 species of fruits, vegetables, nuts, and herbs. The success or failure of his horticultural experiments was inconsequential compared to the example of his stewardship. Jefferson's enthusiasm often outstripped his practical capability; the saga of many horticultural projects, from grape culture to sugar maple plantations, began with dreamy visions that dissolved before the harsh realities of the Virginia climate and an unruly plantation structure. The history of gardening at Monticello is not so much a testament to Thomas Jefferson's horticultural triumphs as it is a reflection of the Jeffersonian spirit—expansive, optimistic, innocent, epicurean; very American.

Landscape Design

In a letter to his granddaughter Ellen in 1805, Jefferson discussed the precise number of fine arts: "Many reckon but 5: painting, sculpture, architecture, music & poetry. To these some have added Oratory ... Others again add Gardening as a 7th fine art. Not horticulture, but the art of embellishing grounds by fancy."[15] Although his ideas on landscape evolved dramatically over his lifetime, Jefferson composed numerous fanciful schemes for the grounds of Monticello. He sketched over twenty designs for ornamental garden structures, some intended for the summit of Montalto ("high mountain"), which towers over Monticello ("little mountain") to the south. He also proposed a series of cascading waterfalls for Montalto and a classical grotto for the north spring at Monticello.[16] Most of these ambitious plans were never realized.

Jefferson toured English gardens in 1786 while serving as minister to France. He wrote upon his return, "the gardening in that country is the article in which it surpasses all the earth, I mean their pleasure gardening."[17] He was impressed by the newest landscape style in which garden designers attempted to imitate the picturesque schemes of eighteenth-century landscape painters and soften the distinctions between garden, park, and English countryside. This visit to England inspired many of Jefferson's ideas for the landscape at Monticello, including the planting of trees in clumps, the informal winding flower walk, and the Grove, or ornamental forest. It also stimulated Jefferson's unifying vision for the landscape—the creation of an ornamental farm, or *ferme ornée*.[18]

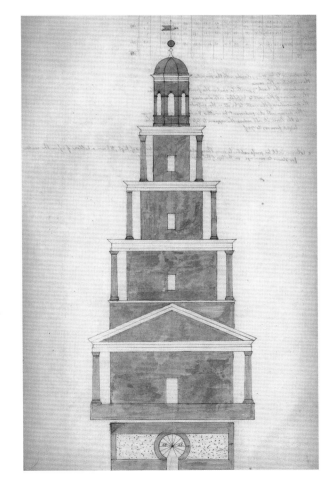

Jefferson's design from the 1770s for an observation tower for Montalto. The windows on the side facing Monticello were to be lower than on the back side so that the line of sight from Monticello would be directed through the building.

PREVIOUS PAGES • Monticello overseer Edmund Bacon recalled, "The grounds around the house were most beautifully ornamented with flowers and shrubbery. There were walks, and borders, and flowers, that I have never seen or heard of anywhere else. Some of them were in bloom from early in the spring until late in the winter."

ABOVE • The "winding walk" flower border. Jefferson wrote his granddaughter Anne on June 7, 1807: "I find that the limited number of our flower beds will too much restrain the variety of flowers in which we might wish to indulge, & therefore I have resumed an idea, which I had formerly entertained, but had laid by, of a winding walk surrounding the lawn before the house, with a narrow border of flowers on each side."

Flower Gardens

The flowers come forth like the belles of the day, have their short reign of beauty and splendor, and retire, like them, to the more interesting office of reproducing their like. The hyacinths and tulips are off the stage, the Irises are giving place to the Belladonnas, as this will to the Tuberoses Etc.; as your Mama has done to you, my dear Anne, as you will do to the sisters of little John, and as I shall soon and chearfully do to you all in wishing you a long, long, good night. [19]

—JEFFERSON TO ANNE CARY BANKHEAD, 1811

Tulip "Apricot Beauty." Jefferson wrote Madame de Tessé, a French friend, in 1803: "When I return to Monticello [from the Presidency] I believe I shall become a florist. The labours of the year, in that line, are repaid within the year, and death, which will be at my door, shall find me unembarrassed in long lived undertakings."

Although there were earlier references to the flower "borders," not until 1807 did Monticello's flower gardens assume their ultimate shape. Anticipating his retirement from the presidency, Jefferson sketched a plan for twenty oval-shaped flower beds in the four corners, or "angles," of the house. Each bed was planted with a different flower, most of which had been forwarded as seeds or bulbs from Philadelphia nurseryman Bernard McMahon, a favorite source of gardening information for Jefferson. The range of flower species planted in 1807 reflected the scope of Jefferson's interests: Old World florists' flowers, local wildflowers, plants of curiosity, fruits of botanical exploration. [20]

In June 1808 Jefferson sent his granddaughter Anne a plan for further plantings for the West Lawn: "I find that the limited number of our flower beds will too much restrain the variety of flowers in which we might wish to indulge, & therefore I have resumed an

The Caracalla bean or snail vine (*Vigna caracalla*).

175

Tulips bloom along the winding walk of the West Lawn in late April. Jefferson wrote to Philadelphia nurseryman Bernard McMahon in 1811: "I have an extensive flower border, in which I am fond of placing *handsome* plants or *fragrant*. Those of mere curiosity I do not aim at, having too many other cares to bestow more than a moderate attention to them."

idea ... of a winding walk ... with a narrow border of flowers on each side. This would give us abundant room for a great variety."[21] The winding walk and the accompanying flower border were laid out in the spring of 1808. By 1812, a need for a more systematic organization required the division of the borders into ten-foot sections, each numbered and planted with a different flower.[22]

The winding, relaxed lines of the walkway reflect Jefferson's interest in the latest, informal style of landscape design. The narrow flower border, or ribbon beds, chopped into ten-foot sections, would not be considered fashionable by modern standards, which celebrate the broad, mixed perennial border as the essence of garden art. The winding walk and border is not a traditional "garden," which usually suggests a room outside, an enclosed retreat. Jefferson's flower beds and borders are exposed to the elements, open to the Piedmont Virginia landscape, intimately balanced with the "workhouse of nature."

A year-round planting plan for the flower gardens has not survived; however, Jefferson would occasionally note specific plantings in the oval or "winding walk" beds in his Garden Book. Many eighteenth-century discoveries were forwarded from the Jardin des Plantes in Paris, and nearly half the documented species planted at Monticello originated with McMahon. Twenty-five percent of the flowers documented at Monticello are North American natives, and the gardens became, in part, a museum of New World botanical novelties.

The flower gardens were cared for by Jefferson's daughters and granddaughters, often assisted by Monticello's most skilled African American slave gardener, Wormley Hughes, or by Jefferson himself, who would help with the design schemes, write labels, or set up a string line to assure straight rows.[23] The flower gardens virtually disappeared after Jefferson's death in 1826, but they were restored by the Garden Club of Virginia between 1939 and 1941. Working with Jefferson's sketches and taking cues from the bulbs that still bloomed 115 years after Jefferson's death, researchers discerned the outline of the winding walk by shining automobile headlights across the West Lawn at night.[24]

The Flower Gardens and fishpond (BELOW) were restored with the help of the Garden Club of Virginia between 1939 and 1941.

Jefferson wrote to Madame de Tessé in 1803: "I own my dear Madame, that I cannot but admire your courage in undertaking now to plant trees. It has always been my passion."

The Trees of Monticello

I never before knew the full value of trees. My house is entirely embosomed in high plane trees, with good grass below, & under them I breakfast, dine, write, read, and receive my company. What would I not give that the trees planted nearest round the house at Monticello were full grown.[25]

—JEFFERSON TO MARTHA RANDOLPH
(FROM PHILADELPHIA), 1793

Jefferson undoubtedly ranked trees at the top of his list of favorite garden plants. Visitors to Monticello were often given tours of the grounds that included a rambling survey of what one guest described as Jefferson's "pet trees."[26] The image of lofty shade trees crowning the summit was consistently evoked by visitors to Monticello.[27] Even in his most functional plantings, Jefferson exploited the ornamental qualities of 160 species of trees. He planted groves of native and exotic trees; "clumps" of orna-mentals adjacent to the house; allées of mulberry and honey locust along his road network of "Roundabouts"; plantations of sugar maple and pecan; and living fences of peach and hawthorn.

Native dogwoods (*Cornus florida*) and redbud (*Cercis canadensis*) in the Monticello woodlands. Anticipating his retirement from the presidency in 1809, Jefferson wrote, "Within a few days I shall bury myself in the groves of Monticello, and become a mere spectator of the passing events."

While serving as minister to France between 1784 and 1789, Jefferson proudly distributed seeds of choice North American trees to friends in Europe, continuing a tradition begun with the earliest European explorers in the New World.[28] He has been described as "the father of American

Jefferson was particularly fond of the willow oak (*Quercus phellos*) and wrote in 1805 that it "combines great singularity with beauty." This contemporary example shades the fish pond on the West Lawn of Monticello.

forestry" for an 1804 planting of white pine and hemlock.[29] His commitment to tree preservation was fervently expressed in comments he allegedly made during a dinner conversation at the President's House: "I wish I was a despot that I might save the noble, the beautiful trees that are daily falling sacrifice to the cupidity of their owners, or the necessity of the poor. … The unnecessary felling of a tree, perhaps the growth of centuries, seems to me a crime little short of murder."[30] Thomas Jefferson's enthusiasm for the arboreal world was unrelenting. Two months before his death, at the age of eighty-three, he designed an arboretum for the University of Virginia. He wrote, "Too old to plant trees for my own gratification I shall do it for posterity."[31]

Only one Jefferson-era tree has survived the inhospitable environment of mountaintop existence. This is a red cedar (*Juniperus virginiana*), a species which, surprisingly, Jefferson said was introduced into Albemarle County.

The Grove

In 1806, Jefferson drew a sketch of Monticello Mountain and designated eighteen acres on the northwestern side as the "Grove," an ornamental forest with the undergrowth removed, the trees pruned and thinned, and the woodland "broken by clumps

In 1806, Jefferson expressed his vision of the ideal American garden, the Grove, to Philadelphian William Hamilton: "Let your ground be covered with trees of the loftiest stature. Trim up their bodies as high as the constitution & form of the tree will bear, but so as that their tops shall still unite & yield dense shade. A wood, so open below, will have nearly the appearance of open grounds."

of thicket, as the open grounds of the English are broken by clumps of trees." He envisioned a pleasure ground where "the canvas at large must be Grove, of the largest trees trimmed very high, so as to give it the appearance of open ground." The Grove also included a planting of ornamental trees in an open area adjacent to the West Lawn.[32] They were chosen for the contrasting textures of their foliage and included wild crabapple (*Malus coronaria*), chinaberry (*Melia azedarach*), umbrella magnolia (*Magnolia tripetala*), aspen (*Populus tremuloides*), and catalpa (*Catalpa bignonioides*). In many ways, the lower or woodland part of the Grove represented Jefferson's ideal American landscape, where "gardens may be made without expense. We have only to cut out the superabundant plants." He said that "under the constant, beaming, almost vertical sun of Virginia, shade is our Elysium."[33]

Although it is uncertain how much of the Grove was actively maintained during Jefferson's lifetime, a project was begun to re-create the concept in 1977. The existing forest was cleared and thinned; young trees, shrubs, and herbaceous flowers planted; and vistas, glades, and thickets introduced as Jefferson envisioned.

Vegetable Garden

I have lived temperately, eating little animal food, and that ... as a condiment for the vegetables, which constitute my principal diet.[34]

—JEFFERSON TO VINE UTLEY, 1819

When Jefferson referred to his "garden," he, like most early Americans, was reserving the term for his thousand-foot-long Vegetable Garden terrace on the southeastern side of his "little mountain." This garden was his chief horticultural achievement at Monticello. Although the garden served as a food source for the family table,

it also functioned as a laboratory where he experimented with seventy different species of vegetables. While Jefferson would grow as many as forty-six bean varieties and twenty-five types of English pea, his use of the scientific method selectively eliminated inferior sorts: "I am curious to select one or two of the best species or variety of every garden vegetable, and to reject all others from the garden to avoid the dangers of mixing."[35]

The garden evolved over many years, beginning in 1770 when crops were grown along the sloping contours of the hillside. Terracing was established by 1809, and by 1812 gardening was at its peak. African American slaves leased by Jefferson from a Fredericksburg farmer hewed the terrace or garden plateau from the side of the mountain. They used a cart and a mule to level the terrace, which was described by one visitor as a "hanging garden."[36] The garden's dramatic setting was enhanced by the pavilion, used by Jefferson as a quiet retreat for evening reading. Reputedly blown down in a violent windstorm by the late 1820s, it was reconstructed in 1984 based upon Jefferson's notes and archaeological excavations.

The main part of the two-acre garden is divided into twenty-four "squares," or growing plots. Species were planted, at least in 1812, according to which part of the plant was being harvested—whether "fruits" (tomatoes, beans), "roots" (beets), or "leaves" (lettuce, cabbage). The site and situation of the garden enabled Jefferson to extend the growing season into the winter months and provided an amenable

microclimate for tender vegetables such as the globe artichoke and winter crops like spinach and endive. Because of favorable air drainage on a small mountaintop, late spring frosts are rare at Monticello and fall's first freeze rarely occurs before Thanksgiving. Jefferson would often gloat over his lowland neighbors' loss of frostbitten fruit, while his own remained unscathed.

Aside from the Garden Pavilion, Jefferson occasionally considered other ornamental features for the terrace. He discussed planting an arbor of different flowering shades of the scarlet runner bean ("purple, red, scarlet, and white"), arranged adjacent rows of purple, white, and green sprouting broccoli, or even white and purple eggplant, and he bordered his tomato square with sesame or okra, a rather unusual juxtaposition of plant textures. Cherry trees were also planted along the "long, grass walk," at the edge of the garden above the wall, to provide shade and spring flowers.[37]

Salads were an important part of Jefferson's diet. He would note the planting of lettuce and radishes every two weeks through the growing season; grow interesting greens like orach, corn salad, endive, and nasturtiums; and plant sesame in order to manufacture a suitable salad oil. While the English pea is considered his favorite vegetable, he also cherished figs, asparagus, artichokes, and such "new" vegetables as tomatoes, eggplant, broccoli, and cauliflower. While Jefferson cultivated common crops like cucumbers, cabbages, and beans, he also prized his sea kale (*Crambe maritima*), a perennial cabbagelike species whose spring sprouts were blanched with pots, then cut and prepared like asparagus. The cultural directions in Bernard McMahon's *Calendar*—for manuring the garden, interplanting lettuce and radishes, and planting cucumbers in hogsheads—were followed diligently in the Monticello garden.

McMahon also sent Jefferson important vegetable varieties such as Leadman's Dwarf pea, Egyptian onion, Early York and Sugarloaf cabbage, red celery, and red globe artichoke.

Jefferson's meticulous notes on the day when peas were sowed or beans harvested suggest he was an active participant in the gardening process. Years after Jefferson's death, one of his former slaves, Isaac Jefferson, recalled, "For amusement he would work sometimes in the garden for half an hour at a time in the cool of the evening."[38] Margaret Bayard Smith, a friend of Jefferson's and a visitor to Monticello, described a portable "frame, or stand, consisting of two upright pieces of about two inches thickness, in which were neat little truss hooks. On these were suspended phials of all sizes, tightly corked, and neatly labelled, containing garden seeds. ... When in his garden this stand could be carried about and placed near him, and if I remember, there

must have near a hundred kinds."[39] Apparently, Jefferson regularly planted the garden himself; however, he was aided by elderly slaves sometimes referred to as the "veteran aids,"[40] who in turn were often led by a series of African American head gardeners: Goliah; Gardener John, who also tended grapes and planted trees that survived well into the second half of the twentieth century; and Great George, who later became Monticello's only African American overseer.

The re-creation of the Monticello Vegetable Garden began in 1979 with two years of archaeological excavations designed to confirm details from the documentary evidence. Archaeologists uncovered the remnants of the stone wall, exposed the foundation of the Garden Pavilion, and discovered evidence for the location of the entrance gate, which then ensured that the squares were laid out according to Jefferson's specifications.

Fruit Garden

Monticello's Fruit Garden, or "Fruitery" as Jefferson called it in 1814, sprawls below the Vegetable Garden. It includes the four-hundred-tree South Orchard; two small vineyards ("northeast" and "southwest"); berry squares of currants, gooseberries, and raspberries; a nursery where Jefferson propagated fruit trees and special garden plants; and "submural beds," where figs and strawberries were grown to take advantage of the warming microclimate created by the stone wall. On the other side of the mountain, Jefferson's North Orchard was reserved for cider apples and seedling peaches (peach trees grown from seed).

Both the Monticello Fruitery (including the South Orchard) and the North Orchard reflected the two distinct forms of fruit growing in eighteenth-century Virginia. The North Orchard was typical of the "field" or "farm" orchards found on

Aerial view of the South Orchard, which Jefferson referred to as the "old nursery." The South Orchard exists today as a repository of Jefferson-era fruit varieties—including the Violet Hative, the oldest nectarine variety still in cultivation—many of which are propagated in the nursery.

most middle-class farms: it was large, on average two hundred trees, and consisted of only apple or peach trees. The fruit was harvested for cider, brandy, or as livestock feed. There is some truth to one historian's tongue-in-cheek remark that it was a significant event when Americans began eating their fruit rather than drinking it.[41] On the other hand, the Monticello Fruitery resembled a gentleman's fruit garden in the Old World horticultural tradition, and was similar to the diverse recreational plantings of other wealthy Virginians such as George Washington. The trees, often planted with small fruits and even ornamentals, were grafted and included a wide spectrum of European varieties and unusual species like apricots and almonds, reserved, according to Jefferson, for the "precious refreshment" of their fancy fruit.[42] The Fruit Garden was cared for sporadically by a series of itinerant European horticulturists, including Scotsman Robert Bailey and Italian Anthony Giannini. They were aided, at least at times, by enslaved African Americans like Great George and Gardener John, who espaliered grapes while Jefferson was in Europe.[43]

NURSERIES

Jefferson had at least two nurseries: the "old nursery" below the garden wall and the terraced "new nursery," which was an extension of the northeast end of the Vegetable Garden. Here

Jefferson mentioned planting thirty-seven varieties of the peach. Based upon the number of trees planted in the Monticello orchards, this could be considered his favorite fruit. Shown here is the Indian Blood peach.

he and Wormley Hughes propagated seeds and cuttings from friends and neighbors. The list of plants grown in the Monticello nurseries included Jefferson's favorite species: thirteen kinds of shrubs, forty-one species of ornamental trees, twenty-six vegetable varieties, six kinds of grasses, eleven nut trees, and fifty-three fruit tree varieties. They were the heart of his pomological, if not horticultural, world. In 1994, a nursery exhibit was re-created on the site of the old nursery.

FENCES

The Fruitery (as well as the Vegetable Garden) was enclosed with a variety of materials during Jefferson's fruit-growing career: board fences, living hawthorn hedges, and even ditches that functioned as cattle guards. The most ambitious enclosure was the paling fence, built by a white carpenter, Mr. Watkins, and three enslaved African Americans in 1808 and 1809. Ten feet high, the fence extended nearly three-quarters of a mile around the entire complex. The palings, or thin boards, were "so near as not to let even a young hare in."[44] Although the paling gates were secured with a lock and key, overseer Edmund Bacon recalled fruit fights that arose when a band of schoolboys, rivals to Jefferson's grandson Thomas Jefferson Randolph, broke down the palings and "did a great deal of damage" by pelting each other with unripe apples and peaches.[45] Although most nineteenth-century orchards were fenced, it was customary for travelers through the Virginia countryside to help themselves to bearing fruit.[46] A sample of the paling fence has been re-created along Mulberry Row.

The Hewes Crab, the most popular apple in eighteenth-century Virginia, was an important cider apple at Monticello.

MONTICELLO
Garden & **Orchard**
ca. 1812

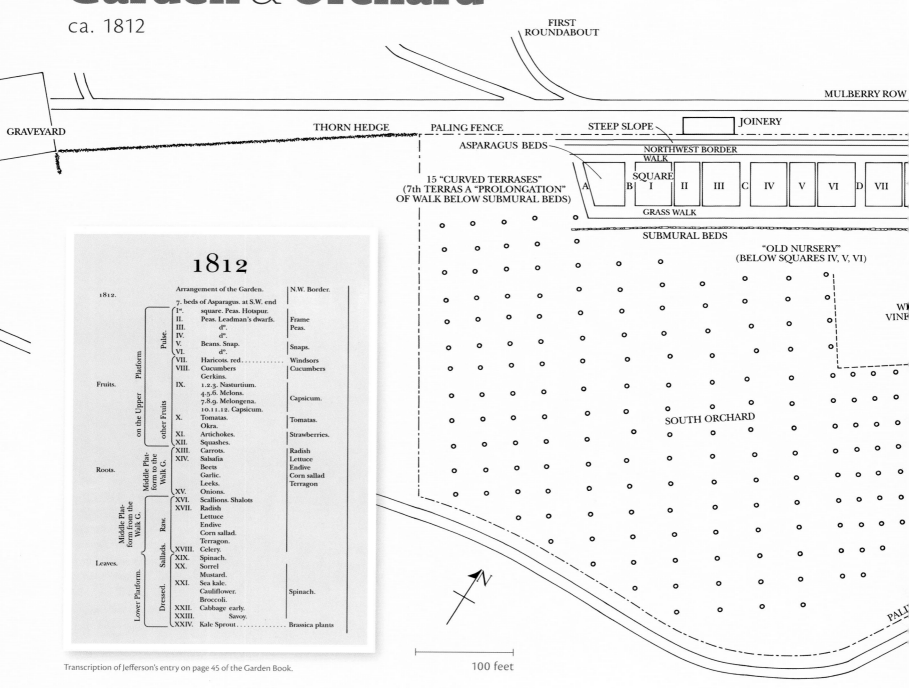

FIRST ROUNDABOUT

MULBERRY ROW

GRAVEYARD

THORN HEDGE   PALING FENCE   STEEP SLOPE   JOINERY

ASPARAGUS BEDS

NORTHWEST BORDER
WALK

15 "CURVED TERRASES"
(7th TERRAS A "PROLONGATION"
OF WALK BELOW SUBMURAL BEDS)

SQUARE

A   B   I   II   III   C   IV   V   VI   D   VII

GRASS WALK

SUBMURAL BEDS

"OLD NURSERY"
(BELOW SQUARES IV, V, VI)

W
VINE

SOUTH ORCHARD

PALI

N

1812

1812.	Arrangement of the Garden.	N.W. Border.
	7. beds of Asparagus. at S.W. end	
	Iˢᵗ. square. Peas. Hotspur.	
	II. Peas. Leadman's dwarfs.	Frame
	III. dº.	Peas.
	IV. dº.	
	V. Beans. Snap.	
	VI. dº.	Snaps.
	VII. Haricots. red	Windsors
	VIII. Cucumbers	Cucumbers
	Gerkins.	
	IX. 1.2.3. Nasturtium.	
	4.5.6. Melons.	
	7.8.9. Melongena.	Capsicum.
	10.11.12. Capsicum.	
	X. Tomatas.	Tomatas.
	Okra.	
	XI. Artichokes.	Strawberries.
	XII. Squashes.	
	XIII. Carrots.	Radish
	XIV. Salsafia	Lettuce
	Beets	Endive
	Garlic.	Corn sallad
	Leeks.	Terragon
	XV. Onions.	
	XVI. Scallions. Shalots	
	XVII. Radish	
	Lettuce	
	Endive	
	Corn sallad.	
	Terragon.	
	XVIII. Celery.	
	XIX. Spinach.	
	XX. Sorrel	
	Mustard.	
	XXI. Sea kale.	Spinach.
	Cauliflower.	
	Broccoli.	
	XXII. Cabbage early.	
	XXIII. Savoy.	
	XXIV. Kale Sprout	Brassica plants

Fruits. — on the Upper Platform — Pulse.
— other Fruits
Roots. — Middle Platform to the Walk G.
Leaves. — Middle Platform from the Walk G. — Raw. — Sallads.
— Lower Platform. — Dressed.

100 feet

Transcription of Jefferson's entry on page 45 of the Garden Book.

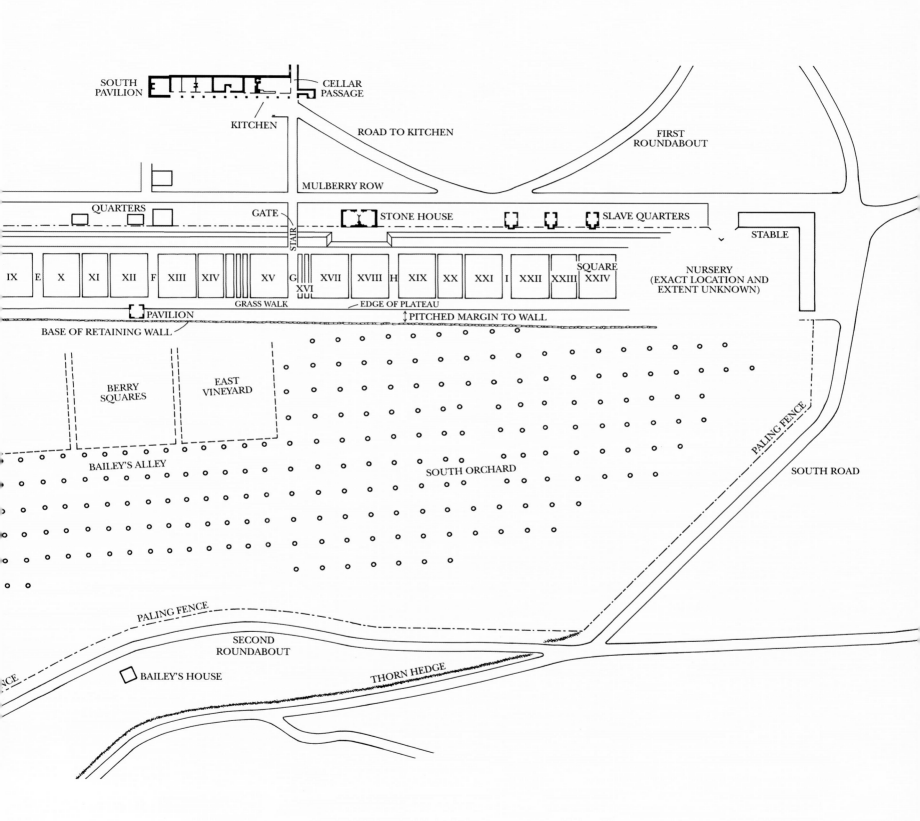

SOUTH
PAVILION

CELLAR
PASSAGE

KITCHEN

ROAD TO KITCHEN

FIRST
ROUNDABOUT

MULBERRY ROW

QUARTERS

GATE

STONE HOUSE

SLAVE QUARTERS

STABLE

STAIR

IX E X XI XII F XIII XIV XV G XVI XVII XVIII H XIX XX XXI I XXII XXIII SQUARE XXIV

NURSERY
(EXACT LOCATION AND
EXTENT UNKNOWN)

GRASS WALK

EDGE OF PLATEAU

PITCHED MARGIN TO WALL

PAVILION

BASE OF RETAINING WALL

BERRY
SQUARES

EAST
VINEYARD

PALING FENCE

BAILEY'S ALLEY

SOUTH ORCHARD

SOUTH ROAD

PALING FENCE

SECOND
ROUNDABOUT

BAILEY'S HOUSE

THORN HEDGE

NCE

SOUTH ORCHARD

Between 1769 and 1814, the South Orchard was planted with as many as 1,031 fruit trees. It was organized into a grid pattern in which grew eighteen varieties of apples, thirty-eight of peaches, fourteen cherries, twelve pears, twenty-seven plums, four nectarines, seven almonds, six apricots, and one quince tree. The earliest plantings, before 1780, reflect the experimental orchard of a young Thomas Jefferson eager to import Mediterranean culture to Virginia and included olives, almonds, pomegranates, and figs. The mature plantings, after 1810, included mostly species and varieties that thrived through central Virginia's hot, humid summers and cold, rainy winters—such as seedling peaches and Virginia cider apples—or else, Jefferson's favorite fancy fruits like the Carnation cherry. The restoration of the South Orchard began in 1981 and was an attempt to re-create his mature, 1811 plan.[47]

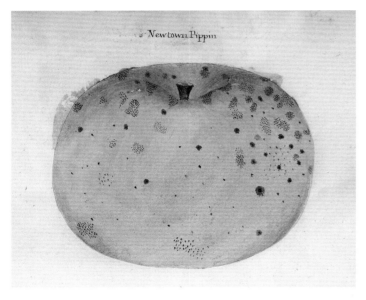

Newtown (or Albemarle) Pippin apple from the second unpublished edition of William Coxe's *A View Toward the Cultivation of Fruit Trees,* circa 1820. The Pippin is America's oldest cultivated horticultural variety, and an industry evolved around Charlottesville in the nineteenth century geared toward this apple's exportation to England.

The peach might be regarded as Jefferson's favorite type of fruit tree; he documented the planting of thirty-eight varieties, and in 1811 the South Orchard included 160 peach trees, far more than any other species. When Jefferson wrote his granddaughter in 1815 that "we abound in the luxury of peach,"[48] he was repeating a theme expressed by colonial fruit growers and even the first natural historians of the New World. At Monticello, peaches were commonly dried and also made into mobby, a form of brandy; in addition, peach trees were planted as living fences around fields and were considered by Jefferson a desirable forestry product. Peach pits also were distributed to Monticello slaves to landscape their cabins a few years after Jefferson died. But Jefferson also tried to assemble a collection of peach varieties for the table, such as the Heath Cling, America's first named peach variety, and the Breast of Venus, which he imported from Italy.[49]

Just as the peach represented the luxurious fertility of the New World, the apple came to symbolize the diversity of America's melting-pot culture. One modern source listed the names of nearly seventeen thousand apple varieties that appeared in nineteenth-century American periodicals. Jefferson's favorite apples included Hewes Crab, a cider apple widely distributed in colonial Virginia, and Taliaferro, "the best cyder apple existing."[50] When comparing the fruits of Europe and America, Jefferson wrote from Paris, "They have no apple to compare with our Newtown Pippin,"[51] which, along with the Esopus Spitzenburg, was his favorite dessert apple.

Jefferson's enthusiasm for his experimental fruit trials was reflected by his proclamations on superior varieties. The Carnation was his favorite cherry, "so superior to all others that no other deserves the name of cherry."[52] The Seckle pear, which originated near Philadelphia, was "the finest pear I've tasted since I left France & equaled the best pear there."[53] The Peach apricot, which he introduced from France, was "the finest fruit which grows in Europe," and the Marseilles fig was "the best in the world."[54] Indeed, Jefferson's 130 varieties of fruit trees represented the finest cultivars available to an early nineteenth-century gardener.

Pesca Poppa di Venere

Ant. Serantoni dis.   Gius: Canacci inc.

Jefferson imported the Breast of Venus peach variety from Italy.

Vineyards

Thomas Jefferson has been described as America's "first distinguished viticulturist," and "the greatest patron of wine and winegrowing that this country has yet had."[55] Although he aspired to make a Monticello-grown wine, his continual replanting of the vineyards suggests a perennial and losing struggle with grape cultivation. But Jefferson was not alone. The successful cultivation in eastern North America of *Vitis vinifera*, the classic European wine species, was virtually impossible until the development of modern pesticides. Native grapes were more effectively grown, yet they produced wine of questionable quality. Jefferson and other New World grape growers were caught between the demands of *V. vinifera* grapes, difficult yet rewarding, and the possibility of native species, like the fox grape (*V. labrusca*) and the Scuppernong variety of the southern muscadine (*V. rotundifolia*), more easily grown in North America.

The two vineyards, northeast (nine thousand square feet) and southwest (sixteen thousand square feet), were ideally sited for grape growing in the heart of the South Orchard below the garden wall. In 1807, Jefferson documented the planting of 287 rooted vines and cuttings of twenty-four European grape varieties, the most ambitious of seven experiments.[56] Many of these *V. vinifera* cultivars had never been grown in North America. Such a varietal rainbow, many of them table grapes, represents the vineyard of a plant collector, an experimenter rather than a serious winemaker. The 1807 plan for the Northeast Vineyard was restored in 1985, the southwest, in 1992. Documentary evidence suggests that Jefferson's vines were "espaliered," or trained over a permanent structure, so the modern re-creation includes a fencelike system built according to an eighteenth-century treatise on grape growing.[57] Jefferson's European varieties were also grafted on the more resilient native rootstock to encourage hardiness and pest resistance.

Sangiovese grape vines in the Southwest Vineyard, restored in 1992. Jefferson's vineyards were planted, and re-planted, numerous times, but the 1807 planting documented the introduction of about twenty-four varieties of *V. vinifera*, or European grapes, and is the most elaborate plan for a vineyard in the United States before 1830.

The Northeast Vineyard at Monticello was restored in 1984 as a varietal
collection of the European table and wine grapes planted in 1807.

Vitus vinifera at Monticello. Jefferson's support for the establishment of an American wine industry and his attempts to grow *V. vinifera* at Monticello have led him to be described as America's "first distinguished viticulturist" and "the greatest patron of wine and winegrowing that this country has yet had."

Wine at Monticello

Thomas Jefferson's knowledgeable and enduring fascination with wine and his pioneering experiments in grape growing at Monticello have endowed him with the reputation as America's "first distinguished viticulturist." Jefferson advised George Washington, John Adams, James Monroe, and James Madison on suitable wines for the White House cellars; kept detailed and often-quoted notes on his wine-tasting travels through Provence, northern Italy, and Germany; and imported extravagant quantities of Europe's most esteemed wines for his own cellars at Monticello and in Washington, where his account books reveal purchases during his eight years of service of over twenty thousand bottles of wine for presidential dinners.

Jefferson served wine after dinner daily, and numerous visitors to both Monticello and the President's House attested to the spirited conversations that ensued, whether about politics or about Jefferson's multifaceted interests in architecture, art, music, or literature. His own vibrant refrains on wine animate the story: when he said, "No nation is drunken where wine is cheap," or, "Wine from long habit has become an indispensable for my health," he provided inspiration for the wine enthusiast and grower alike. Jefferson believed that his native land had the "soil, aspect, and climate of the best wine countries" and that "We could, in the United States, make as great a variety of wine as are made in Europe, not exactly of the same kinds, but doubtless as good." Perhaps most importantly, Jefferson's curious promotion of American-made wine and his association with other pioneering grape growers stimulated experimental viticulture in the New World.

ABOVE • This labeled Madeira decanter, excavated from the dry well site of the Monticello kitchen yard, dates from the 1760s. English-made, it is decorated with a cartouche and grapevine motifs. After his death, twelve decanters were recorded in an inventory; some of these might have been those that he had shipped back from France in 1790.

LEFT • This *seau crénelé*, a crenellated vessel for rinsing wine glasses, was part of a service decorated with a *guirlande de barbeaux* (cornflower garland) made at the royal French porcelain factory at Sèvres exclusively for the use of Louis XVI at Versailles. How Jefferson obtained this and a *sucrier* (sugar bowl) from the same service is not known.

ABOVE • Jefferson purchased many styles of stemware between 1767 and 1821, including these English lead-glass examples with a band of wheel-cut sprig and oval engraving. By 1826, only seventeen wine glasses were mentioned in the household inventory made after Jefferson's death.

ABOVE • Chateau Lafite was one of the four vineyards in the Bordeaux region of France that Jefferson noted as of the first quality when he toured the region in May 1787.

ABOVE • The wine cellar at Monticello has been restored to reflect Jefferson's interest in wine both as a connoisseur and as a viticulturist. Fine wine was a feature of his table when he was in public office and at Monticello. In 1774, he had grapes planted at Monticello; however, there are no records of successful wine production. His cellar was stocked primarily with wines ordered from Europe.

Center for Historic Plants

A fitting tribute to Jefferson's interest in garden plants, and the natural result of the restoration of Jefferson's gardens at Monticello, was the opening of the Center for Historic Plants in 1987. This educational garden center is devoted to the collection, preservation, and distribution of plants known in early American gardens. The program focuses on Thomas Jefferson's horticultural interests and the plants he grew at Monticello, but it also covers the broad history of plants cultivated in America by including varieties documented through the nineteenth century, as well as choice North American plants, a group of special interest to Jefferson himself. The Garden Shop, open year-round, is located at Monticello's David M. Rubenstein Visitor Center. Historic plants, heirloom seeds, and books on the history of garden plants are available through the shop. The center's nursery is located at one of Jefferson's quarter farms, Tufton, and includes growing facilities and display gardens for its collection of historic roses, Dianthus, and irises.

Globe centaurea, *Centaurea macrocephala*, was among the uncommon perennials sent to Monticello by Philadelphia nurseryman, Bernard McMahon, in 1812.

Cow's Horn Okra
Hibiscus esculentus

'Bath Cos' Lettuce
Lactuca sativa

own Dutch' Lettuce
Lactuca sativa

Scarlet-runner Bean
Phaseolus coccineus

West Indian Gherkin
Cucumis anguiria

Prickly-seeded Spinach
Spinacea oleracea 'Prickly-seeded'

ppo Lettuce
potted Aleppo'

Costoluto Genovese Tomato
Lycopersicon lyco;
'Costoluto Gem

Yellow Arikara Bean
Phaseolus vulgaris 'Yellow Arikara'

Anne Arundel Melon
Cucumis melo 'Anne Arundel'

ill Cowpea
hippoorwill'

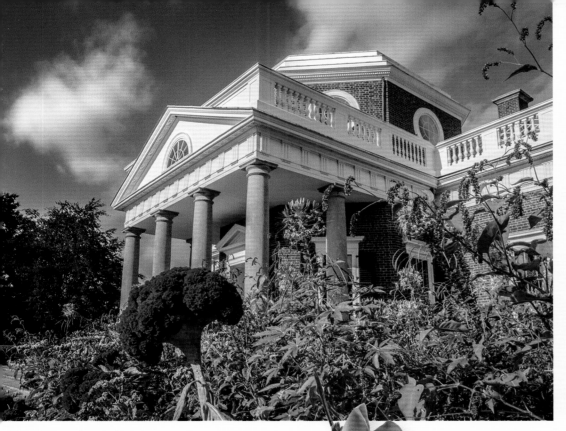

ABOVE • Herbaceous peony.

"I have often thought that if heaven had given me choice of my position and calling, it should have been on a rich spot of earth, well watered, and near a good market for the productions of the garden. No occupation is so delightful to me as the culture of the earth, and no culture comparable to that of the garden. Such a variety of subjects, some one always coming to perfection, the failure of one thing repaired by the success of another, and instead of one harvest a continued one thro the year. Under a total want of demand except for our family table, I am still devoted to the garden.

But tho an old man, I am but a young gardener."

—Jefferson to Charles Willson Peale, August 20, 1811

ABOVE • Black cohosh (*Cimicifuga racemosa*) is among the native plants grown in the gardens of Monticello and included among the collections of the Center for Historic Plants.

ABOVE • French, or stick-a-dove, lavender (*Lavandula stoechas*) was grown in Virginia gardens as early as 1735.

LEFT • Hyacinth bean (*Dolichos lablab*) flowers are a visual highlight in the garden late in summer.

205

Archaeology at Monticello

BY FRASER NEIMAN

Director of Archaeology at Monticello

Archaeological research plays an important role in the attempt to recover a more complete picture of the complex social and economic community that flourished at Monticello during Thomas Jefferson's lifetime. Monticello's archaeologists have investigated the belowground traces of the plantation outbuildings that once stood along Mulberry Row and the orchards and Vegetable Garden to the south of it. During this work, thousands of artifacts were recovered, along with the remains of vanished buildings, fences, and other landscape features.

Archaeological research at Monticello is reaching beyond the confines of the mountaintop with the first systematic archaeological survey of the two thousand acres of land that formed the core of Jefferson's five-thousand-acre plantation. Among the key findings thus far is the location of at least one slave burial ground on the property. Another emphasis of Monticello's present archaeological work is reexamining our long-held assumptions about Mulberry Row, a reminder that understanding our history is an ongoing, changing process.

ABOVE • Archaeologists revealed the original brick floor of Monticello's first kitchen after excavating the three feet of fill deposited in the South Pavilion cellar around 1809. In the gaps between the bricks they found food remains, including eggshell fragments and fish scales.

RIGHT • An ebony ring and cowrie shell hint at the persistence of African materials and usages at Monticello. In seventeenth- and eighteenth-century West Africa, cowries had monetary and symbolic value and were used for personal adornment, hung on a string, or sewn to clothing. Pierced European and American coins represent an African American reinvention of the tradition. They also document slaves' access to cash and participation in the regional economy.

BELOW • Fashionable ceramics, like the Chinese porcelain pictured here, are common on slave domestic sites at Monticello and elsewhere. Research suggests that much of this material was purchased by enslaved people, and not given to them by their owners. Variation in ceramic styles among sites hints at both an interest among some slaves in stylish ceramics and varying amounts expended to acquire them.

RIGHT · Housing for enslaved people was a prominent feature of the Monticello mountaintop landscape from 1769 to 1826. On Mulberry Row, most slaves lived in clay-chinked log cabins with dirt floors, clay-lined wood chimneys, and unmortared stone foundations. The plans of the buildings changed significantly over time. Archaeology reveals that slave houses built in the 1770s and 1780s had larger rooms, about 260 square feet (NEAR RIGHT). After 1790, room sizes declined to about 160 square feet (Building "s") (FAR RIGHT). While a few rooms had a single, small subfloor pit, most rooms lacked them entirely. The shift probably represents an increase in the influence some slaves had over their housing situations, and their preference to live in smaller, family-based groups.

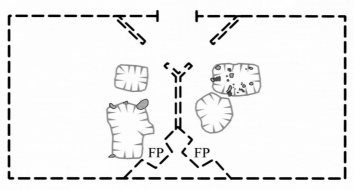

"Negro Quarter" (ca. 1770–80)

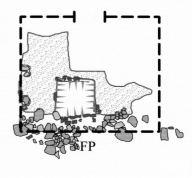

Building "s" (ca. 1790–1830)

Digital Archaeological Archive of Comparative Slavery

The Digital Archaeological Archive of Comparative Slavery (DAACS) is an award-winning research collaboration based at Monticello. DAACS fosters inter-site, comparative archeological research on slavery in the Chesapeake, the Carolinas, and the Caribbean. Since its founding by the Thomas Jefferson Foundation in 2000, DAACS has helped scholars from different disciplines use archaeological evidence to advance our understanding of the slavery-based societies that evolved in the Atlantic world. Today the DAACS website (daacs.org) provides scholars and the public open access to data on over 3 million artifacts and the contexts from which they were excavated. Not only does DAACS nurture research through sharing high-quality data, but the program also provides fellowships, training, and access to software through the DAACS Research Consortium (daacsrc.org). DAACS is supported by major grants from the Andrew W. Mellon Foundation, the National Endowment of the Humanities, and Monticello donors.

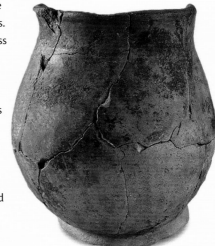

Support for the Restoration of Monticello

The Thomas Jefferson Foundation gratefully acknowledges these individuals and organizations for their leadership gifts and grants since 2010 in support of Monticello's restoration:

Mountaintop Project

David M. Rubenstein

Mr. and Mrs. John H. Birdsall

Robert H. Smith Family Foundation

W. L. Lyons Brown III

Stuart R. Brown

Cary Brown Epstein

The Joseph and Robert Cornell Memorial Foundation

The Mary Morton Parsons Foundation

Sally and Joe Gladden

The Manning Family Foundation

Jan Karon

Mr. Ronald S. Kossar

Caterpillar

The Beirne Carter Foundation

Tommy and Kemp Hill

Cabinet

Grady and Lori Durham and Family

Bed Chamber

David and Susan Goode and Family

Library

Christopher J. Toomey

Martha Jefferson Randolph's Room

Ms. Charlotte Moss and Mr. Barry Friedberg

Dining Room

Polo Ralph Lauren

Mulberry Row

Fritz and Claudine Kundrun

National Endowment for the Humanities

Richard S. Reynolds Foundation

The Mars Family

The Cabell Foundation

Mr. and Mrs. Richard A. Mayo

Stable

The Sarah and Ross Perot, Jr. Foundation

Kitchen Road

Garden Club of Virginia

Notes

Short Titles and Abbreviations

DLC   Library of Congress, Washington, D.C.

GB   Betts, Edwin M., ed., *Thomas Jefferson's Garden Book.*
      Philadelphia: The American Philosophical Society, 1944.
      Reprint, Charlottesville: Thomas Jefferson Memorial
      Foundation, Inc., 1999.

MB   Bear, James A., Jr., and Lucia C. Stanton, eds., *Jefferson's
      Memorandum Books: Accounts, with Legal Records and
      Miscellany, 1767-1826.* Princeton: Princeton University
      Press, 1997.

MHi   Massachusetts Historical Society, Boston

Nichols   Nichols, Frederick D., *Thomas Jefferson's Architectural
      Drawings*, 5th ed. Charlottesville: Thomas Jefferson
      Memorial Foundation, 1984.

PTJ   Boyd, Julian P., et al., eds., *The Papers of Thomas Jefferson.*
      Princeton: Princeton University Press, 1950–.

PTJ:RS   Looney, J. Jefferson, et al., eds., *The Papers of Thomas
      Jefferson: Retirement Series.* Princeton: Princeton
      University Press, 2004–.

Randall   Randall, Henry S., *The Life of Thomas Jefferson.* New
      York: Derby and Jackson, 1858.

Smith   Smith, Margaret Bayard, *The First Forty Years of
      Washington Society.* Edited by Gaillard Hunt. New
      York: Charles Scribner's Sons, 1906. Reprint, New York:
      Frederick Ungar Publishing Co., 1965.

ViU   Special Collections, Alderman Library, University of
      Virginia, Charlottesville

Visitors   Peterson, Merrill D., ed., *Visitors to Monticello.*
      Charlottesville: University Press of Virginia, 1989.

The Plantation: A Day in the Life
(pp. 1-39)

1   TJ to Isaac A. Coles, 27 August 1814, MHi.

2   Jefferson, *Notes on the State of Virginia*, 166-168.

3   TJ to George Washington, 14 May 1794, *PTJ*, 28:75;
    TJ to Francis Willis, 15 July 1796, *PTJ*, 29:153.

4   TJ to Henry Knox, 1 June 1795, *PTJ*, 28:374.

5   TJ to Thomas Mann Randolph, 18 August 1795, *PTJ*, 28:438.

6   TJ to John Milledge, 5 June 1811, *PTJ:RS*, 3:637.

7   TJ to James Adair, 1 September 1793, *PTJ*, 27:4.

8   TJ to Stevens T. Mason, 27 October 1799, *PTJ*, 31:222.

9   TJ to William Johnson, 10 May 1817, *GB*, 572.

10 TJ to Benjamin Austin, 9 January 1816, in Merrill D. Peterson, ed.,
    Thomas Jefferson: Writings (New York: Library of America, 1984), 1371.

11 Madison Hemings recollections, 13 March 1873, in Annette Gordon-
    Reed, *Thomas Jefferson and Sally Hemings: An American Controversy*
    (Charlottesville: University Press of Virginia, 1997), 247.

12 TJ to John W. Eppes, 30 June 1820, in Edwin Morris Betts, ed.,
    Thomas Jefferson's Farm Book (Princeton: Princeton University
    Press, 1953; reprint, Charlottesville: Thomas Jefferson Memorial
    Foundation, Inc. 1999), 45.

Thomas Jefferson's Essay in Architecture
(pp. 41-85)

1   TJ to Elbridge Gerry, Philadelphia, 13 May 1797, *The Writings of
    Thomas Jefferson*, ed. Albert Ellery Bergh (Washington, D.C.: Thomas
    Jefferson Memorial Association, 1903), 9:381. A version of this essay
    appeared as "Thomas Jefferson and the Art of Living Out of Doors,"
    in *The Magazine Antiques*, April 2000, 594-605.

2   TJ to Reverend Hatch, Monticello, 12 May 1822, Coolidge Collection of Jefferson Manuscripts, MHi.

3   "Charlottesville-Monticello-Mr. Jefferson-University of VA., From the Letters from a Valetudinarian," *Niles National Register*, 6 July 1839, 301.

4   TJ to Benjamin Henry Latrobe, Monticello, 10 October 1809, *The Correspondence and Miscellaneous Papers of Benjamin Henry Latrobe*, ed. John C. Van Horne and Lee W. Formwalt (New Haven: Yale University Press, for the Maryland Historical Society, Baltimore, 1984-1988), 2:777.

5   *MB*, 1:76.

6   The most comprehensive checklist of the drawings is found in Frederick D. Nichols, *Thomas Jefferson's Architectural Drawings*, 5th ed. Many of the drawings were reproduced in Fiske Kimball, *Thomas Jefferson Architect* (Boston: privately published, 1916; reprint, New York: DaCapo Press, 1968).

7   Jefferson cites Palladio as early as 1769, with entries dating from 1769 in his 1767 Memorandum Book. At the time, he owned an English translation of Palladio's *I Quattro libri dell'architettura* by Giacomo Leoni: *The Architecture of A. Palladio* (London, 1742). For this and other editions of Palladio's works owned by Jefferson, see E. Millicent Sowerby, *Catalogue of the Library of Thomas Jefferson*, 5 vols. (Charlottesville: University Press of Virginia, 1983) and William B. O'Neal, *Jefferson's Fine Arts Library* (Charlottesville: University Press of Virginia, 1976).

8   Marquis de Chastellux, *Travels in North America in the Years 1780, 1781, and 1782*, trans. Howard C. Rice, Jr. (Chapel Hill: University of North Carolina Press, 1963). Quoted in *Visitors*, 12.

9   Ibid.

10 TJ to George Wythe, 23 October 1794, *PTJ*, 28:181.

11 For a description of the Hôtel de Langeac, the town house that Jefferson rented in Paris, see Howard C. Rice, Jr., *Thomas Jefferson's Paris* (Princeton: Princeton University Press, 1976), 51-54.

12 Cited in Jefferson's notebook for the remodeling of the house. See Nichols, nos. 139, pp. 2-4; 145, p. 14; and 146, p. 16.

13 See Jefferson's building notebook, Nichols, nos. 140, p. 7 and 147-b, pp. 5, 6.

14 TJ to John Brown, 5 April 1797, *PTJ*, 29:346.

15 Ibid.

16 Jefferson identifies the nursery in his notebook for the remodeling of the house: Nichols, nos. 139, p. 4; 144, p 11; 147-b, pp. 1, 2. The Appendix is identified on a floor plan by Jefferson's granddaughter Cornelia Randolph produced shortly after his death; ViU, accession no. 5385-ac, Nichols, no. 563-2. Both are identified in John W. Eppes to TJ, 6 November 1801, *PTJ*, 35:579.

17 TJ to Mann Page, Monticello, [1796], MHi.

18 TJ to Benjamin Henry Latrobe, Monticello, 8 September 1805, *Correspondence ... of Benjamin Henry Latrobe*, 2:140. Blinds were also designed for the large Dining Room skylight.

19 Smith, 72.

20 Ibid., 71.

21 Ellen Randolph Coolidge, quoted in Randall, 3:347.

22 Isaac Weld, *Travels through the States of North America* (London, 1799), quoted in *Visitors*, 19.

23 The location of the workbench is shown on Cornelia Randolph's floor plan; ViU, accession no. 5385-ac, Nichols, no. 563-2. For references to making models see James A. Bear, Jr., ed., *Jefferson at Monticello* (Charlottesville: University Press of Virginia, 1967), 84. For references to carpenters' tools and making small things out of metal see p. 18.

24 Nichols, no. 144. On the back of a memorandum (Nichols, no. 147-l verso) dated 24 September 1804, Jefferson included "the Aviary" among the work "reserved" for his slave joiner John Hemmings.

25 Smith, 385.

26 TJ to Étienne Lemaire, Monticello, 25 April 1809, *PTJ:RS*, 1:162.

27 See Nichols, no. 147-p; TJ to James Dinsmore, Washington, 28 December 1806, DLC; and TJ to James Dinsmore, Washington, 6 February 1808, MHi.

28 See Nichols, no. 147-m.

29 Ibid., no. 147-q. No. 147-p, verso is probably the preliminary study. The Venetian Porches were completed in 2000. Mesick, Cohen, Wilson, Baker, Albany, New York were the architects;

fabrication was by Gaston & Wyatt, Charlottesville, Virginia; hardware by The Colonial Williamsburg Foundation and Cersley, Masonry. Installation was by Monticello staff members Robert Self, Architectural Conservator, and Robert Newcomb, Restoration Specialist, both of whom also constructed the corner terraces. The re-creation was based on nineteenth-century photographs (some computer-enhanced); Jefferson's notes and drawings; and physical evidence that confirmed such things as the alignment of the louvered work against the brick walls and the plaster ceiling line. Although green paint was found on the brickwork, it proved to date from the end of the nineteenth century. However, a louvered slat from Jefferson's period was found in the attic with its paint layers intact. The primer is white lead and the first finish coat is verdigris mixed with a small amount of *terre verte* and fillers (probably calcium carbonate). The paint analysis was by Susan Buck, Historic Paint and Architectural Services, Newton Center, Massachusetts. The T. David Fitz-Gibbon Charitable Trust funded the reconstruction of the corner terraces, and the Florence Gould Foundation funded the re-creation of the Venetian enclosures.

30 Nichols, nos. 147-p, 147-r.

31 TJ to William Hamilton, Washington, July 1806, DLC.

32 Copy by Ellen Randolph Coolidge of her letter to an unknown recipient, Boston, 27 January [1833 or 1834], Trist Papers, ViU, 6696.

33 Henry Home, Lord Kames, *Elements Of Criticism* (Edinburgh, 1762; reprint, New York: Johnson Reprint, 1967), 3:313. Jefferson knew of this work by 1771 when he recommended it to Robert Skipwith. See TJ to Skipwith, 3 August 1771 in *PTJ*, 1:79. For the importance of *Elements of Criticism* to Jefferson, see the many references in Eleanor D. Berman, *Thomas Jefferson Among the Arts* (New York: Philosophical Library, 1947).

34 For the "angular portals," see Nichols, no. 147-l. Jefferson notes that work on "the 3. remain[ing] Angular Portals" is "reserved for J. Hemings." The fact that three portals are mentioned implies that there were at least four—hence the likelihood that they are at the four corners of the house. The violet bed is identified on Cornelia Randolph's floor plan, Nichols, no. 563-2.

35 Sarah N. Randolph, *The Domestic Life of Thomas Jefferson Compiled from Family Letters and Reminiscences by His Great-Granddaughter* (1871; reprint, Charlottesville: University Press of Virginia, for the Thomas Jefferson Memorial Foundation, 1978), 332. The original

terrace roofs and railings were gone by the time of the earliest known photographs of the house. The present restoration dates from 1938-41. The Chinese railings are based on an understanding of Jefferson's intent as well as on several visitors' descriptions and a few early engravings. These views, at best, show a Chinese railing on only a short section of the North Terrace. The patterns used for the restoration are based on railings depicted in early engravings of Jefferson's buildings at the University of Virginia.

36 Bear, *Jefferson at Monticello*, 72.

37 Randall, 3:347.

38 Randolph, *Domestic Life of Thomas Jefferson*, 347.

39 Randall, 3:336.

40 Randolph, *Domestic Life of Thomas Jefferson*, 337.

41 Nichols, no. 147-s.

42 Ibid., nos. 147-l verso and 147-m.

43 Ibid., no. 147-ff verso.

44 Ibid., no. 147-ff verso.

45 Ibid., no. 147-ll.

46 See TJ to James Dinsmore, Washington, 8 June 1805, Herbert R. Strauss Collection, Newberry Library, Chicago.

47 Randall, 3:331.

48 [Margaret Bayard Smith], *Winter in Washington; or, Memoirs of the Seymour Family* (New York: E. Bliss and E. White, 1824), 221. Also in B. L. Rayner, *Sketches of the Life, Writings, and Opinions of Thomas Jefferson* (New York: A. Francis and W. Boardman, 1832), 524.

49 TJ to Benjamin Henry Latrobe, Monticello, 10 October 1809, *PTJ:RS*, 1:595-6. Also quoted in *Correspondence ... of Benjamin Henry Latrobe*, 2:777. As far as we know Latrobe never visited Monticello.

50 TJ to Martha Jefferson Randolph, Philadelphia, 7 July 1793, *PTJ*, 26:445-6.

A Look Inside Monticello
(pp. 87-121)

1 TJ to Angelica Schuyler Church, 27 November 1793, *PTJ*, 27:449.

2 Martha Jefferson Randolph to Ellen Randolph Coolidge, 18 September 1825, ViU, 9090.

3 Unidentified daughter to Martha Jefferson Randolph, n.d., ViU, 9090.

4 George Ticknor, 7 February 1815, *Visitors*, 62.

5 Ibid.

6 John French, ca. 1825, James. A. Bear, compiler, "Descriptions of Monticello, 1780-1826," vol. 1, Research Report, Jefferson Library, Thomas Jefferson Foundation (hereafter, TJF).

7 Randolph, *Domestic Life of Thomas Jefferson*, 347.

8 George Ticknor, *Life, Letters, and Journals of George Ticknor*, 2 vols. (Boston: James R. Osgood and Company, 1876), 1:36.

9 Virginia Randolph Trist to Ellen Randolph Coolidge, 3 September 1825, ViU, 9090.

10 Martha Jefferson Randolph to Ellen Randolph Coolidge, 2 August 1825, ViU, 9090.

11 Martha Jefferson Randolph to Ellen Randolph Coolidge, 1 September 1825, ViU, 9090.

12 Daniel Webster, *Visitors*, 90.

13 Smith, 69.

14 Ibid., 48.

15 Ticknor, *Life, Letters, and Journals*, 1:36.

16 William Parker Cutler and Julia Perkins Cutler, *Life Journals and Correspondence of Rev. Manasseh Cutler* (Cincinnati, 1888), 2:71-2.

17 Daniel Webster, *Visitors*, 98.

18 Benjamin Henry Latrobe to Mrs. Latrobe, 24 November 1802, *Correspondence ... of Benjamin Henry Latrobe*, 1:232.

19 Smith, 67-68.

20 Francis Calley Gray, *Visitors*, 57.

21 Elizabeth Lindsay Gordon cited in Armistead Churchill Gordon, *William Fitzhugh Gordon: A Virginian of the Old School: His Life, Times, and Contemporaries* (NY: Neale, 1909), 58.

22 Cornelia Jefferson Randolph to Ellen Randolph Coolidge, 26 August 1825, ViU, 9090.

23 Ellen Randolph Coolidge to Henry S. Randall, 16 May 1857, ViU, 9090.

24 TJ to N. Burwell, 14 March 1818, cited in Randall, 447.

25 Bear, *Jefferson at Monticello*, 136n.

26 Sir Augustus John Foster, *Visitors*, 39.

27 TJ to John Adams, 10 June 1815, in Lester J Cappon, ed. *The Adams-Jefferson Letters* (Chapel Hill: University of North Carolina Press, 1987), 443.

28 John Edwards Caldwell quoted in William M.E. Rachal, ed., *A Tour through a Part of Virginia in the Summer of 1808.* (NY: H C Southwick, 1810; reprint, Richmond: Dietz Press, 1951), 28.

29 Smith, 49-50.

30 Ibid.

31 Ibid., 71.

32 Bear, *Jefferson at Monticello*, 18.

33 Smith, 71.

34 George Tucker, *The Life of Thomas Jefferson, Third President of the United States* (Philadelphia: Carey, Lea & Blanchard, 1837), 190.

35 Daniel Webster, *Visitors*, 98.

36 Virginia Jefferson Randolph to Nicholas P. Trist, 5 June 1823, Nicholas P. Trist Papers, DLC, reel 2/frame 172.

Furnishing Monticello:
Jefferson as Consumer and Collector
(pp. 123-157)

1 Howard C. Rice, Jr., *Thomas Jefferson's Paris* (Princeton: Princeton University Press, 1970), 15.

2 *MB*, 1:557.

3 TJ to Samuel Osgood, 5 October 1785, *PTJ*, 8:590.

4 For more information on the *marchands merciers,* see Carolyn Sargentson, *Merchants and Luxury Markets: The Marchands Merciers of Eighteenth-Century Paris* (London: Victoria and Albert Museum in association with the J. Paul Getty Museum, 1996).

5 *MB,* 1:565.

6 Ibid.

7 Joseph Spence, *Polymetis: Or an Enquiry Concerning the Agreement between the Works of the Roman Poets, and the Remains of the Antient Artists. Being an Attempt to Illustrate Them Mutually from One Another.* (1747; reprint, New York: Garland Publishers, 1976), v.

8 TJ to John Trumbull, 30 August 1787, *PTJ,* 12:69.

9 TJ to Madame de Bréhan, 19 March 1789, *PTJ,* 14:656.

10 TJ to Madame de Corny, 30 June 1787, *PTJ,* 11:509.

11 TJ to John Page, 4 May 1786, *PTJ,* 9:445.

12 Lucia C. Stanton, in *The Worlds of Thomas Jefferson at Monticello*, ed. Susan R. Stein (New York: Harry N. Abrams, Inc., 1993), 350.

13 TJ to Nathaniel Colley, "Mem. for Capt. Colley to have made in London for Th.J," 16 November 1789, *PTJ,* 15:546.

14 TJ to James Madison, 10 January 1791, *PTJ,* 18:480.

15 TJ to John Adams, 25 April 1794, in Paul Leicester Ford, ed., *The Writings of Thomas Jefferson*, 12 vols. (New York: G.P. Putnam's Sons, 1904-1905), 6:505.

16 TJ to Charles Willson Peale, 6 October 1805, DLC.

17 George Ticknor, *Life, Letters and Journals*, 1:34.

18 TJ to Benjamin Rush, 16 January 1811, in Ford, *Writings,* 11:168.

19 Thomas Jefferson, *Notes on the State of Virginia* (London, 1787; reprint, with notes, William Peden, ed., Chapel Hill: University of North Carolina Press, 1955), 24 (page references are to reprint edition).

Gardens of Monticello
(pp. 159-209)

1 Edwin M. Betts, ed., *Thomas Jefferson's Garden Book* (Philadelphia: The American Philosophical Society, 1944; reprint, Charlottesville: Thomas Jefferson Memorial Foundation, Inc., 1999).

2 Benjamin S. Barton, *Transactions of the American Philosophical Society* (1793, 3:334-347), reprinted in *GB,* 172.

3 TJ, "Memorandum of Services," ca. September 1800, PRJ, 32:124.

4 Jefferson, *Notes on the State of Virginia.*

5 For more information, see *GB,* 108-132.

6 TJ to Madame de Tessé, 26 October 1805, *GB,* 305-306.

7 Bernard McMahon, *The American Gardener's Calendar* (Philadelphia: B. Graves, 1806).

8 *GB,* 538–539.

9 Ellen Randolph Coolidge to Henry Randall, n.d., in Randall, 3:346-347.

10 TJ to Martha Randolph, 21 July 1793, *PTJ,* 26:546.

11 TJ to Thomas M. Randolph, 1 May 1791, *PTJ,* 20:340.

12 TJ to Charles Willson Peale, 20 August 1811, *PTJ:RS,* 4:93.

13 TJ to Timothy Matlack, 19 October 1807, *GB,* 352.

14 Dumas Malone, *Jefferson the President: Second Term, 1805–1809* (Boston: Little Brown and Co., 1974), 291-292.

15 TJ to Ellen Randolph, 10 July 1805, *GB,* 303–304.

16 For more information on Jefferson and landscape architecture, see Frederick D. Nichols and Ralph E. Griswold, *Thomas Jefferson Landscape Architect* (Charlottesville: University of Virginia Press, 1978).

17 TJ to John Page, 4 May 1786, *PTJ,* 9:445.

18 For more information on Jefferson's trip to England, see *GB,* 110–114, and Samuel A. Roberson, "Thomas Jefferson and the Eighteenth-Century Landscape Movement in England," Ph.D. diss., Yale University, 1974. For more information about the *ferme ornée*, see William L. Beiswanger, "The Temple in the Garden: Thomas Jefferson's Vision of the Monticello Landscape," in John Dixon

Hunt, ed., *British and American Gardens in the Eighteenth Century* (Williamsburg, Va.: Colonial Williamsburg Foundation, 1984), 170-188.

19 TJ to Anne Cary Bankhead, 26 May 1811, in *PTJ:RS*, 3:633.

20 Jefferson's plan of the oval and round flower beds, April 1807, reproduced and the text transcribed in *GB*, 334–335.

21 TJ to Anne Cary Randolph, 7 June 1807, and 16 February, 1808, *GB*, 349, 363-364. See also sketch reproduced in plates XXIV and XXV.

22 "Calendar for this year, 1812," March 28 1812, *GB*, 474.

23 Ellen Randolph Coolidge to Henry Randall, n.d., in Randall, 3:346–347.

24 Hazelhurst Perkins, unpublished diary of Monticello garden restoration, TJF.

25 TJ to Martha Randolph, 7 July 1793, in *PTJ*, 26:445-446.

26 Francis Hall, 1816, in "Descriptions of Monticello, 1780–1826," TJF.

27 For more information, see "Descriptions of Monticello, 1780–1826," and "Descriptions of Monticello, 1826–Present," TJF.

28 *GB*, 105-147.

29 Garden Book entry for April 12, 1804, *GB*, 291.

30 Smith, "The President's House Forty Years Ago," in *Godey's Lady's Book* (November, 1843), 216.

31 TJ to Constantine Rafinesque, 9 October 1822, in *GB*, 604.

32 Jefferson's notes accompanying a sketch of the top of Monticello Mountain, ca. 1778, ViU, N-61 (K-34).

33 TJ to William Hamilton, July 1806, *GB*, 322-324; and TJ, "Hints to Americans Travelling in Europe," enclosed in letter to John Rutledge, Jr., 19 June 1788, *PTJ*, 13:269.

34 TJ to Vine Utley, 21 March 1819, DLC.

35 TJ to Bernard McMahon, 13 January 1810, *PTJ:RS*, 2:140.

36 TJ to Lewis W. Dangerfield, 5 September 1806, MHi; TJ to Edmund Bacon, 24 November 1807, Henry E. Huntington Library, San Marino, California; Tucker, *Life of Thomas Jefferson*, 473.

37 "Calendar for this year, 1812," 12 April 1812; 28 March 1812; Kalendar, 1812; 16 April 1812; Garden Book notation for 6 June 1810; *GB*, 474, 471, 425.

38 Isaac Jefferson in Bear, *Jefferson at Monticello*, 18.

39 Smith, "Recollections of a Visit to Monticello," *Richmond Enquirer*, 18 January 1823.

40 TJ to Maria Jefferson Eppes, 11 April 1802, in Edwin M. Betts and James A. Bear, Jr., eds., *The Family Letters of Thomas Jefferson* (Charlottesville: University Press of Virginia, 1966), 201.

41 Liberty Hyde Bailey, *The Apple Tree* (New York: The Macmillan Company, 1922), 62.

42 TJ to James Madison, 15 May, 1794, *PTJ*, 28:76.

43 Thomas Jefferson's instructions to [overseer] Richard Richardson, December 1794, in *The New York Times*, 14 April 1923.

44 TJ to Mr. Watkins, 27 September 1808, *GB*, 377.

45 Bear, *Jefferson at Monticello*, 87-88.

46 Peter Hatch, *The Fruits and Fruit Trees of Monticello: Thomas Jefferson and the Origins of American Horticulture* (Charlottesville: University Press of Virginia, 1998), 29.

47 For more information, see Hatch, *Fruits and Fruit Trees*.

48 TJ to Martha Randolph, 31 August 1815, *GB*, 547.

49 Hatch, *Fruits and Fruit Trees*, 79–82.

50 TJ to James Barbour, 5 March 1816, *GB*, 555–556.

51 TJ to Reverend James Madison, 28 October 1785, *PTJ*, 8:681-683.

52 TJ to James Barbour, 5 March 1816, *GB*, 556.

53 TJ to Timothy Matlack, 1 March 1806, *GB*, 352.

54 TJ to Charles Clay, 1 March 1806 and TJ to William Drayton, 7 May 1789, *GB*, 317, 143.

55 Thomas Pinney, *A History of Wine in America* (Berkeley: University of California Press, 1989), 129.

56 TJ, 1807 Vineyard Plan, in Weather Memorandum Book, Historical Society of Pennsylvania, Philadelphia.

57 Edward Antill, "An Essay on the Cultivation of the Vine, and the Making of Wine, Suited to the Different Climates in North-America," *Transactions of the American Philosophical Society* (Philadelphia: 1771, 2d ed.) 1:201-210.

Photo Credits

The Foundation acknowledges the support of the Massachusetts Historical Society and the University of Virginia for their assistance and generosity in supplying a host of Jefferson-related documents and photographs for *Thomas Jefferson's Monticello*. We would also like to thank individual lenders (listed below) for their generosity in sharing their artifacts with the Foundation and with the readers of this book.

All photos are copyright Thomas Jefferson Foundation, Inc. (TJF), except as otherwise noted.

Cover	Shaking Hands, TJF
Endsheets	Monticello: mountaintop (plat), 1809, by Thomas Jefferson (n225; K169) Courtesy of the Massachusetts Historical Society
ii	Jack Looney, TJF
iv-v	Robert Llewellyn, TJF
vi	Peggy Cornett, TJF
vii	Library of Congress, Manuscript Division
viii	Jack Looney, TJF
ix	Walter Smalling, TJF
xii	Walter Smalling, TJF
xv	Hollande/Obama: Jack Looney, TJF
xvi	John Lewis: Jack Looney, TJF
	Rubenstein/Meacham: Jack Looney, TJF
xix	Detail from *Thomas Jefferson* by Jean-Antoine Houdon, 1789, gift of the Gilder Lehman Collection, photographed by Edward Owen, TJF
xxiv	Gardiner Hallock, TJF
1	Monticello: re: crop rotation, undated, by Thomas Jefferson (N230; K169e), courtesy of the Massachusetts Historical Society
2	Nailrod: Robert Owen, TJF
	Record of nailmakers' work: Library of Congress, Manuscript Division
4	"An Overseer Doing His Duty, Near Fredericksburg, Virginia" by Benjamin H. Latrobe, courtesy of the Maryland Historical Society
	Bottom two photos: Edward Owen, TJF
5	Stable: Jack Looney, TJF
	Snow: Peggy Cornett, TJF
6-7	RenderSphere, LLC, TJF

8	Courtesy of William Andrews Clark Memorial Library, University of California, Los Angeles
9	Lily Fox-Bruguiere, TJF
10	Merchant mill: Oliver Evans, *The Young Mill-Wright and Miller's Guide*, 1795
12-13	Shaking Hands, TJF
14	Keith Damiani, TJF
15	Library of Congress, Morgan Collection of Civil War Drawings
16	Wellcome Library, London, Wellcome Images, Creative Commons
17	Robert Self, TJF
18	Farm Book, 1774-1824, page 152, by Thomas Jefferson, courtesy of the Massachusetts Historical Society
19	Courtesy of Mason County Museum, Maysville, Kentucky
20	Jack Looney, TJF
22	Edward Owen, TJF
24	Philip Beaurline, TJF
26	Isaac Granger Jefferson daguerreotype: courtesy Special Collections, University of Virginia Library, Charlottesville, Virginia
27	Jack Looney, TJF
28	Henry Martin photo: courtesy Special Collections, University of Virginia Library, Charlottesville, Virginia
	Robert Hemings's deed of manumission: 24 December 1794, courtesy Special Collections, University of Virginia Library, Charlottesville, Virginia
29	Library of Congress, Manuscript Division
30	Cook's room: Michael Bailey, TJF
	Bell: Courtesy of Moorland-Spingarn Research Center, Howard University, photographed by Edward Owen
	Kitchen inventory: Library of Congress, Manuscript Division
31	Elizabeth-Ann Isaacs: *Ebony,* November 1954
	Peter Fossett: Wendell P. Dabney, *Cincinnati's Colored Citizens*, Cincinnati, 1926
	Robert Hughes: Photo courtesy of the Union Run Baptist Church, Keswick, Virginia
	Portrait of Colonel John Wayles Jefferson: Courtesy of the Museum of Wisconsin Art

Index

Boldface type *indicates a photograph or illustration.*

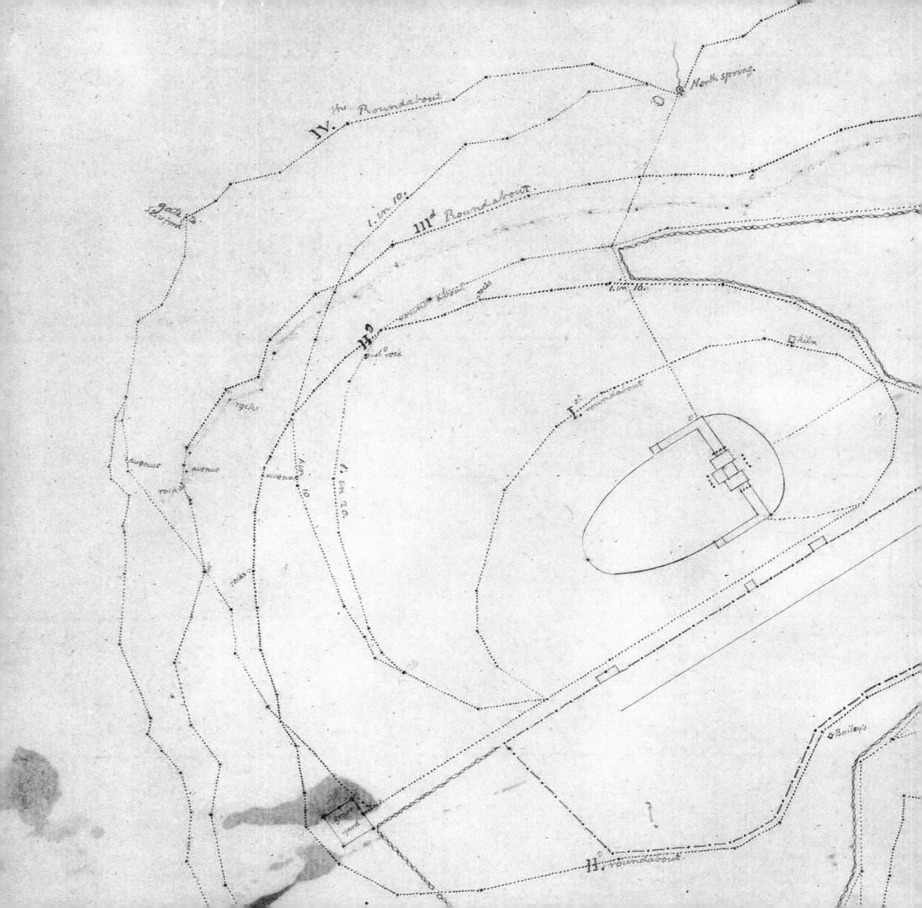